Observer's Books

NATURAL HISTORY
Birds · Birds' Eggs · Wild Animals · Zoo Animals
Farm Animals · Freshwater Fishes · Sea Fishes
Tropical Fishes · Butterflies · Larger Moths
Insects and Spiders · Pond Life · Sea and Seashore
Seashells · Dogs · Horses and Ponies · Cats
Trees · Wild Flowers · Grasses · Mushrooms
Lichens · Cacti · Garden Flowers · Flowering Shrubs
House Plants · Vegetables · Geology · Weather
Astronomy

SPORT
Association Football · Cricket · Golf · Coarse Fishing
Fly Fishing · Show Jumping · Motor Sport

TRANSPORT
Automobiles · Aircraft · Commercial Vehicles
Motorcycles · Steam Locomotives · Ships
Small Craft · Manned Spaceflight
Unmanned Spaceflight

ARCHITECTURE
Architecture · Churches · Cathedrals

COLLECTING
Awards and Medals · Coins · Postage Stamps
Glass · Pottery and Porcelain · Furniture

ARTS AND CRAFTS
Music · Painting · Modern Art · Sculpture
Sewing

HISTORY AND GENERAL INTEREST
Ancient Britain · Flags · Heraldry
European Costume

TRAVEL
London · Tourist Atlas GB

The Observer's Book of

POTTERY AND PORCELAIN

MARY AND GEOFFREY PAYTON

ILLUSTRATED IN
LINE AND HALF-TONE
WITH EIGHT PAGES OF COLOUR PLATES

FREDERICK WARNE & CO LTD
FREDERICK WARNE & CO INC
LONDON : NEW YORK

To
'*The Girls*' *of Yarcombe*

LIBRARY OF CONGRESS CATALOG
CARD NO. 73-80247

ISBN 0 7232 1518 9

Printed in Great Britain by
William Clowes & Sons, Limited
London, Beccles and Colchester
1596·1276

CONTENTS

LIST OF COLOUR PLATES

PREFACE

This book is primarily for the amateur collector, but those who enjoy just browsing among the unattainable in museums, country-house collections and salerooms have not been forgotten. The widespread and still growing interest in pottery and porcelain has been reflected in the number of requests our publishers have had in recent years for just such a book.

As we draw nearer to the end of the 20th century, most 18th-century pottery and porcelain has passed beyond the reach of the average collector—though there are exceptions, e.g. the smaller items of First Period blue-and-white Worcester, and the earliest New Hall. Thus the attention of dealers and their customers alike has of necessity become increasingly focused on the 19th and even the 20th century. Many of us would very much like to possess a Chelsea Red Anchor figure—but its price would now run to many hundreds of pounds.

For these reasons fine 18th-century porcelains and the fascinating field of early English pottery have been treated as of historical rather than practical interest to the active collector today, and relatively greater space has been given to later and less expensive items, e.g. Staffordshire figures, that offer wider scope and variety to those whose urge to collect is restrained by the harsh facts of budgetary considerations.

For browser and collector alike, an introductory chapter outlines the development of ceramics from the earliest times, while the main part of the book deals, in alphabetical order, with the various potteries and the main types of collectable items with, where possible, aids to recognition and warnings of pitfalls. In addition there are appendices listing useful dates, useful books, notable collections and the more important marks, and an index to facilitate quick reference.

Our thanks are due to Shirley Hartshorne of Yarcombe for taking all the colour photographs and most of the black-and-white photographs not credited to others.

South Zeal

MARY PAYTON
GEOFFREY PAYTON

INTRODUCTION

Cross-references: Words in SMALL CAPITALS indicate references to main entries which appear in their appropriate alphabetical place.

Ceramics (from the Greek for 'pottery') is the only satisfactory term that covers both porcelain and pottery; 'china' no longer has a precise meaning and is best avoided unless qualified (as in 'bone china'). **Porcelain** is a fine variety that you can see through (usually) if you hold it up to the light. **Pottery** is of much coarser texture, and (normally) opaque; the two main types are **earthenware**, which is porous, and **stoneware**, which is not. The differences between these forms arise from the materials used, the temperature at which they are fired in the kiln, and the proportion of vitreous (i.e. glassy) elements in them.

POTTERY

As every gardener knows, clay is sticky (and thus easily moulded or plastic) when wet, bone-hard when dried by the sun—and that was how the first pottery was made, perhaps 8000 years ago, the shaped pots being left to bake under the Mesopotamian sun.

For it was in this region, it is thought, that man first turned from a roving life of hunting and food-gathering to the settled life of the farmer—a change known as the Neolithic Revolution. Since those days successive generations of potters have learnt how to solve many problems: how to generate enough heat to bake the clay harder (from sun-heat to today's 1400° C is a long step); how to make the finished product less easily breakable, less porous, smoother in texture and surface, more attractive to look at, lighter in weight.

The first step forward was to 'fire' the clay over an open wood fire. Porosity, before the discovery of glazing, was dealt with by covering the pot with a gum and resin varnish. The urge to decorate came surprisingly early, first as dots and lines scratched with a stick, developing into chevrons and geometrical patterns. Colour decoration also came early; a polychrome plate found in Iraq has been dated to 4500 BC; while from Susa, a future Persian capital, came a painted terracotta cup and vase, made a thousand years later, and a beaker with finely executed geometrical design. An early example of glazing, also from Susa, occurs on a vase decorated with rosettes (c. 2500 BC).

Meanwhile the Neolithic Revolution had seeped east and west, to reach both China and Western Europe by, at the latest, 2000 BC, the probable date of pottery well decorated with coloured clays, found in Kansu, an early centre for Chinese pottery. Not much later the Egyptians were making their finest glazed vitreous earthenware, and the Bronze Age Beaker Folk in England were leaving a legacy of beakers finely decorated with herring-bone and cross-hatched designs.

The potter's wheel may have reached England not long before the Romans, who brought with them the craft of making glossy red earthenware. Little pottery seems to have been made during the English Middle Ages; there are examples of coloured lead glaze, e.g. on a jug splendidly decorated in low relief with a stag-hunting scene (c. 1300). A rich dark-brown glaze is also found on redware from the great Cistercian houses such as Fountains Abbey.

The 16th century saw the introduction to England from the Netherlands of tin-enamelled earthenware, later called DELFTWARE; the chief centres of its manufacture in the 17th century were Lambeth and Bristol. In the same century another type of earthenware was made in Kent and Staffordshire; this was SLIPWARE, which is of interest more as a style of decoration than as a stage in the development of pottery.

By this time a new factor was arising to spur on pottery development—the rapid spread of the vogue for the new exotic hot drinks, tea and coffee. The first London 'Cophee House' opened in 1652; in 1660 Pepys could record: 'I did send for a cup of tee (a China drink) of which I never had drank before'. But a century later imports exceeded 5 million lb a year. At first it was served in the red stoneware teapots and cups imported with the tea from China by the Dutch and English East India Companies, or in the mysterious and expensive blue-and-white porcelain which, noted Sir Thomas Browne c. 1650, 'according to common belief is made of Earth'. The problem was to make a cheaper substitute.

While Continental potters tried to make porcelain, in England the challenge was met by an Oxford M.A., John Dwight of FULHAM, who in 1684 took out a patent for fine STONEWARE (which he called porcelain), and by the Elers brothers (see ELERS WARE) who, at Fulham from c. 1690 and thereafter in Staffordshire, produced similar wares, including fine redware. Elers ware was unglazed but, since it was fired at high temperature (1200°C), was not porous and, unlike delftware, not vulnerable to hot liquids. Dwight also developed a white SALTGLAZE stoneware, which was nearer to Chinese porcelain in colour and could be similarly decorated. It was in this material that Staffordshire and other potters first made the little figurines of horsemen etc. in a style which was also adapted to earthenware by ASTBURY and WHIELDON. The Elers were accused of stealing Dwight's secrets, and one of the Astburys is said likewise to have stolen the Elers' secrets and applied them to the manufacture of his lead-glazed stoneware.

Various factors contributed to a steady improvement in stoneware which made it very different from the coarse grey stonewares of 16th-century Germany and Flanders. The addition to the clay of calcined flints (variously attributed to Dwight, Astbury or Heath) gave stability in the kiln, durability and whiteness. About 1715 the important discovery was made that Devon and Cornwall yielded a particularly pure china-clay, used ever since in Britain and exported all over the world, as the 'slag-heaps' that disfigure the neighbourhood of St Austell and elsewhere testify. Ball-clay, a fine white pipeclay originally imported in ball form from Devon and Dorset, was added to give greater plasticity and strength; and felspar was added as a flux. The remaining problem was surface texture. Unglazed stoneware (except for the Dwight-type redware) was too rough; lead glaze detracted from appearance; saltglaze was better, but nevertheless had an orange-skin surface.

In the 1720s some genius (again, possibly, an Astbury) discovered that the stoneware ingredients, if fired at the much lower temperature of 750°C, produced a useful cream-coloured earthenware. Whieldon used this with tortoiseshell and mottled colour glazes. A clear lead glaze was then evolved which, applied to this ware as a liquid dip and replacing salt-glaze, produced an ideal body that, under the name of CREAMWARE, came to displace saltglaze and other wares not only in Britain but on the Continent and in America for a century. Its further development was mainly due to Wedgwood (see QUEEN'S WARE, PEARL-WARE) and the LEEDS POTTERY. It had the advantage of being both light and strong, and it was attractive to look at, whether painted, transfer-printed or left un-decorated.

Between 1767 and 1785 Wedgwood also took the lead in developing new forms of stoneware, notably BLACK BASALT, JASPER WARE and CANEWARE, and in the following century Spode developed STONE CHINA (a form of earthenware, as was MASON'S PATENT IRON-STONE CHINA).

STAFFORDSHIRE FIGURES had also come to the fore; these might be regarded as the poor man's Chelsea. Some of the best of these were made by the WOOD FAMILY, led by Ralph Wood (from c. 1754). They made many other things, e.g. TOBY JUGS, but a line of potters working on a small scale specialized in figures only, notably the BOCAGE figures of the WALTON SCHOOL (c. 1806–46), and the less cosy products of Obadiah SHERRATT.

Outstanding developments in 19th-century pottery included Staffordshire BLUE-AND-WHITE, which was at its best 1815–40, the late Prattware POT-LIDS of mid-century, Minton's MAJOLICA, DOULTON's stoneware decorated by the Barlow family, and the grotesqueries of MARTINWARE (1870s), leading up to the STUDIO POTTERY movement which is still with us.

PORCELAIN

Hard-paste ('true') porcelain was first made in China, in the 9th century AD (T'ang Dynasty); it was produced by mixing china-clay (*kaolin*, a pure white clay formed by the decay of felspar, the chief constituent of granite) with china-stone (*petuntse*, less fully decomposed felspar). These were fused together by firing in a kiln, first at about 900°C, then dipped in glaze and refired at about 1300°C; this resulted in a translucent body under a tight-fitting glaze. The china-stone bound the clay particles together and imparted translucency; the high temperature vitrified the whole body, i.e. gave it the consistency of glass.

China exported its porcelain wares (especially blue-and-white) to Europe in ever increasing quantity from the 16th century, mainly through the English and Dutch East India Companies; by 1700 there was a vast trade in them, and wares of the Ming Dynasty (1368–1644) were particularly prized. As they were very expensive, Europeans tried hard to discover the secret of hard-paste manufacture, but it was not until 1710 that the King of Saxony's captive alchemist Böttger found out how to make it, using local materials.

The Meissen factory (just outside Dresden, the Saxony capital) was set up to make this. Although the king tried to keep the formula secret, it was soon leaked to Vienna (an early example of industrial espionage) and later elsewhere. In England William Cookworthy discovered the requisite ingredients in Cornwall, thus enabling true hard-paste porcelain to be made, by a formula which passed successively from Plymouth (Cookworthy, 1768) to Bristol (Champion,

1774) and New Hall (1781–1812), and CAUGHLEY/ Coalport imitated New Hall. Hard-paste porcelain is today standard in most countries other than England.

In the meantime **soft-paste porcelain** had been produced in Europe as early as *c.* 1575; this was the Medici porcelain made, for a few years only, in Florence. A fine creamy variety had also been evolved in France, at Rouen (1673) and St Cloud (near Paris). In the post-Meissen period French soft-paste wares were made at Chantilly, Mennecy, Vincennes and (1756–1804) Sèvres; Italian at Capodimonte (Naples) from 1745; English at Chelsea (1745), Derby, Longton Hall and, in modified form (see below), Bow.

The essential difference between hard and soft paste lies in the ingredients used. In soft-paste (also called 'artificial' or 'frit') porcelain a glassy mixture of sand or calcined flint with potash or lead was substituted for china-stone, and various locally available white clays for the Chinese type of china-clay; the result (at its best) was a creamy or ivory porcelain. The glassy mixture is technically known as a **frit** (from the Italian for 'fried'), i.e. a fusion of materials, finely ground, which gives stability to the body paste; a glassy frit is also the basis of glazes, giving them their waterproofing quality. In contrast to hard-paste, soft-paste porcelain was first fired at a higher temperature (about 1100°C) to produce a translucent **biscuit** stage (i.e. fired but unglazed); the biscuit was then dipped in glaze and refired at about 900°C.

Both hard and soft paste porcelains had their disadvantages, tending to distort or collapse in the kiln; a high proportion of such 'wasters' (i.e. rejects) naturally increased the price of the saleable products. Early soft-paste wares were also liable to crack under a sudden change of temperature, e.g. when tea was poured into a tea-bowl, and were sometimes soft enough to be scratched by spoon or knife.

The substitution of **soapstone** (steatite) for china-clay produced a soft-paste body better able to survive the rigours of the kiln and changes in temperature; it was denser, harder, much heavier, and it vitrified at a lower kiln temperature. Soapstone, a silicate of magnesia found in Cornwall, was first used at Lund's Bristol factory (1749), then by Liverpool (up to the 1770s), Worcester (1751–1820s) and Caughley (1775–1799).

Still more rewarding was the discovery that **bone-ash,** from calcined ox-bones, also reduced kiln collapses. Added to *soft-paste* ingredients, it produced a whiter, more plastic body. Bow was the first to use Thomas Frye's patent for this (1749), followed by Lowestoft (1757), Chelsea (gold anchor, 1758), Chelsea-Derby and Liverpool.

Finally, bone-ash was added to *hard-paste* ingredients to form the first **bone china** ('non-frit china'), marketed by Josiah Spode (1794); china-stone, china-clay and bone-ash were mixed in the proportions 1 : 1 : 2. The product was very white, translucent and plastic, more durable and much cheaper. The formula was adopted by Flight & Barr (Worcester) from *c.* 1800 and soon afterwards by Derby, Rocking-ham, Coalport, Minton etc., quickly becoming, as it remains, the standard type of English translucent china, nearer to hard than soft paste (but strictly speaking neither), and almost exclusively English.

Another variant was **felspar china**, in which felspar was substituted for part of the china-stone in the ingredients of bone china; this increased hardness, durability, transparency and resistance to kiln temperatures, and was cheaper. Spode first tried it (*c.* 1815) and Coalport used it shortly afterwards. A rather less durable type of felspar china was used on the Continent. (Stone china and ironstone china are types of earthenware.)

Distinguishing hard and soft

It is sometimes suggested that this is easy—for true soft paste can be scratched with a knife or a nail-file which makes no mark on hard paste. But this test is not wholly reliable (e.g. early Worcester and other soapstone china resists steel) and in any case it would be a bold customer who picked up a piece in an antique shop and started filing it to see what happened—and an unpopular one. A broken piece can be identified easily enough, as hard paste fractures like glass or flint, leaving clean, sparkling edges of compact texture, while a soft paste fracture is granular, like fine lump sugar. (Hard-paste New Hall is an exception to this.) Scratching an unglazed area will ruin the finger-nail if hard paste, but may mark it if it is soft. The only certain test is chemical analysis.

A more practical method is to examine the general appearance and feel of the piece, and these are largely determined by the type of glaze, the subject of the next section.

POTTERY AND PORCELAIN

Glazes

Glaze is applied to a porcelain or pottery body to make it waterproof, enhance colour and add brilliance to its surface. Glazes may be translucent, opaque or coloured.

Hard-paste porcelain was given a **felspar glaze** made of powdered china-stone mixed with lime, potash, sand or quartz. Being of similar composition, body and glaze fused intimately together. Pottery and soft-paste porcelain were treated in various ways. Early English soft-paste and earthenwares such as creamware were coated in a transparent glassy **lead glaze** (sand or silica fused with a lead oxide), a process which caused lead poisoning among the workmen. The proportion of lead, at first as much as 40%, was therefore steadily reduced, and as early as 1820 Coalport won an award for introducing an excellent **leadless glaze**, using felspar. In delftware calcined tin oxide was added to the lead glaze, giving an opaque white finish. **Salt glaze** was used on some pottery; salt was thrown into the kiln at high temperature and fused with the clay (see SALTGLAZE). Glazes may be stained by the metallic content of the clay, natural or introduced; **coloured glazes** were used on earthenware by Thomas Whieldon, Ralph Wood and others.

The glazed surface of most hard-paste porcelain (except Plymouth) has a brilliantly white hard glitter and a cold touch; any overglaze decoration stands out and can be felt. By contrast, soft paste looks and feels warmer and softer, feeling like unused toilet soap or (especially New Hall) candles; overglaze decoration sinks into the glaze and the overall effect of subdued colours and mellow richness is preferred by many to the relative garishness of, for example, German porcelain. In figures the difference is particularly noticeable; the thin close-fitting glaze on hard paste makes for finer detailed modelling, while the thicker

richer soft-paste glaze produces softer unsharp outlines, often with pools of surplus glaze forming in
hollows.

Imperfections

Crazing, a network of fine cracks in the glaze, was a
feature of some early soft-paste porcelain and of pottery, caused by the warping of lead glazes that did not
blend properly with the body. It did not occur on
hard paste nor, notably, on First Period Worcester.
Crazing is not a sure sign of age as it can be faked.

Warping also caused another soft-paste feature, **firecracks**, formed during firing. Though sometimes
quite large, these are acceptable to collectors who
would unhesitatingly reject a piece with the finest of
hair-cracks or the smallest of chips. Some early
English soft paste had internal air-bubbles or variations
in the thickness of the glaze, causing variations in translucency seen, when held to the light, as 'pinholes' or
'moons' (early Chelsea, Longton Hall).

Colour decoration

This may be overglaze, underglaze or by use of coloured
glazes. **Overglaze decoration** used elaborately
prepared mixtures of pigments from metallic oxides
with (at first) flint-glass, to form what were virtually
colour glazes; these are technically known as **enamel
colours**. Each colour might have to be fired separately, at specific but relatively low temperatures (in the
700–950° C. range). On soft-paste porcelain, during
the firing, the enamels melted and sank into the softened
glaze. On hard-paste this was not so; the layers of
colour stand 'proud', can be felt, and are vulnerable
to chipping. Decoration in several colours is called
polychrome. Among the sources of enamel colours

are manganese (purple), copper or chromium (green), iron (red), uranium or antimony (yellow). The shades of colour differ with the temperature used.

To avoid the high cost of hand-painting, TRANSFER-PRINTING, a purely English speciality, was introduced by Robert Hancock at Worcester (1756) and later became standard practice elsewhere; designs were engraved on copper plate from which impressions were taken on specially treated very thin paper, and transferred to the already glazed wares.

In **underglaze decoration** the colours were painted (or transfer-printed) on to the unglazed biscuit, and had therefore to withstand much higher firing temperatures. At first the easiest colour to manage at high temperatures was cobalt blue—hence the prevalence of BLUE-AND-WHITE from the Ming period onwards, and its popularity for English printed tablewares, since the glaze protected the decoration from wear. Underglaze blue transfer-printing, pioneered by Worcester *c.* 1760, was adopted almost everywhere except Chelsea.

Gilding

Various techniques have been used, e.g. **honey gilding** (from *c.* 1755) in which gold leaf was ground up with honey and, after firing at a low temperature, burnished. This gave a dull finish; a brassy finish resulted from **mercury gilding** ('best' gold), introduced *c.* 1790, in which the mercury of a gold amalgam was vaporized. From the 1850s '**bright**' or **liquid gold** was used on some earthenwares, e.g. flatbacks. It was a very thin film of colloidal gold, so brilliant that it needed no burnishing; but it did not wear well.

AN A–Z OF POTTERY
AND PORCELAIN

Adams family　A line of Staffordshire potters stretching from 1657 to today.　Among the most notable were William of Tunstall and Greengates (1779–1805), who made Wedgwood-style blue jasper with white reliefs—the blue being more violet than Wedgwood's; his son Benjamin (1805–12), who made high-quality blue transfer-printed pearlware; and William of Stoke (1804–29), who made blue-printed earthenware with appropriate scenes (e.g. the 'Landing of Columbus' set) for the U.S. market.　Other products include black basalt and fine stoneware.

Agate ware　Earthenware made to look like agate by building up irregular layers of clays coloured white, brown, green and blue; it was lead glazed.　It differs

1　AGATE WARE
Staffordshire cat with
brown striated body
and blue glaze
markings (*Christie's*)

from tortoiseshell ware (see WHIELDON WARE) as the veining is in the clay, not the glaze. Agate table-wares were made by Thomas Whieldon from about 1740 and then by Wedgwood and other Staffordshire potters until *c.* 1820; small figures of cats (fig. 1), pugs, birds etc. were also popular.

Alcock, Samuel (worked *c.* 1828–59) A Staffordshire manufacturer of pottery and porcelain with a wide range of wares, notably Rockingham-style table-wares, moulded jugs in Parian ware, and blue-and-white.

Animals and birds Interesting collections can be built up from the immense variety of these, in pottery and porcelain. Porcelain examples, often Meissen-inspired, were made by most 18th-century manu-facturers, particularly Chelsea and Bow; some now fetch extremely high prices, especially the 'Chelsea toys' (see GIRL-IN-A-SWING FACTORY). Native species predominate, usually pets, farm animals or sporting (both the hunter and the hunted). Pugs seem to have been the favourite pet, cosily ensconced on tasselled cushions. Pointers and setters standing over game are the commonest sporting subjects. 'Rockingham' poodles and sheep with coats of shredded porcelain are not now thought to have come from Rockingham. A Derby pair of figures, often seen in pottery versions, are the 'Welsh' Tailor and Wife mounted on goats (an oddly popular animal in those days) carrying every-thing but the kitchen sink; despite the name, it is copied from Meissen. Classical themes are repre-sented by Leda and the Swan, Europa and the Bull, numerous paw-on-globe lions (copied from Roman sculpture; fig. 123) and groups inspired by Aesop's

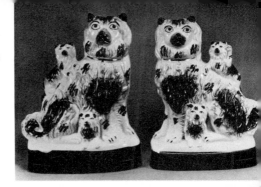

2 ANIMALS AND BIRDS Pair of Staffordshire pottery figures of 'comforter' dogs with puppies. *c.* 1860 (*Oliver-Sutton Antiques*)

JUMBO

3 ANIMALS AND BIRDS Staffordshire pottery figure of Jumbo, *c.* 1885 (*Oliver-Sutton Antiques*)

fables. Gold Anchor Chelsea added BOCAGES to some models. Longton Hall produced some fine equestrian pieces. Tureens were made in the form of a pheasant, boar's head, rabbit, hen and chickens etc., sometimes life-size.

A noteworthy modern development at Worcester (which made few animals and birds in its early days) is a series of limited-edition studies of birds in their natural habitat, inspired by Audubon's *Birds of America* but also modelled from life. These were made from 1935 by Charles Doughty's daughter Dorothy.

Potters covered a much wider range, in earthenware, brown stoneware, saltglaze and creamware, from at least the 17th century. WHIELDON WARE, the WALTON SCHOOL, SHERRATT, LEEDS (especially the horses) and COW-CREAMERS account for many. The exotic is represented by a Chinese-inspired boy on water-buffalo group (Whieldon), dromedaries, lions (with their tamers), the London Zoo's first giraffe (1830; 'I don't believe it', said one lady firmly) and its famous Jumbo (1860; fig. 3), as popular an idol as Chi Chi. From bear-baiting days come numerous Nottingham and Derby brown stoneware beer jugs in the form of a sitting bear hugging a terrier, the head detachable as a cup; also owl-jugs—both coated with shredded clay. Equally odd are the early 19th-century Sussex pig-mugs, also with detachable heads; these are still made. Cats are relatively rare; most notable are those in solid agate (fig. 1). Dogs abound, especially the greyhound *couchant*, with or without its kill, and including Waterloo Cup winners; and dalmatians, the Regency carriage-dogs. The 'comforter' (fig. 2), an extinct breed of spaniel-like lap-dog, was immensely popular from the 1850s, sitting up, wearing a gold chain and a puzzled expression, and decorated with red or lustred spots; it was made in pairs, large for the hearth or small for the mantelpiece (see STAFFORDSHIRE FIGURES, VICTORIAN). And, of course, there are the MARTINWARE 'birds' that never were on

4 ANIMALS AND BIRDS Staffordshire saltglaze enamelled finch, c. 1755 (*City Museum, Stoke-on-Trent*)

5 ANIMALS AND BIRDS Staffordshire Walton-style deer (*Mary Payton Antiques*)

6 ANIMALS AND BIRDS Staffordshire zebra, c. 1850 (*Mary Payton Antiques*)

land or sea. The most popular birds, apart from the farmyard, seem to have been finches (fig. 4) and the canary. See also figs. 5 and 6.

Apostle jugs Relief-decorated stoneware jugs so called after a gothic design registered (1842) by the Staffordshire potter Charles MEIGH (fig. 9), which showed a frieze of the apostles standing in niches beneath pointed arches. Similar jugs were made by others, including Samuel Alcock and Ridgway, and most bear the maker's mark.

Armorial china From the 18th century there was a vogue for dinner sets, punch-bowls etc. embellished with the family arms (genuine or assumed). At first these were made and decorated in China, sometimes with quaint results as the Chinese were inclined to rearrange armorial details for aesthetic reasons, or even to copy instructions to the decorator on to the plate. See CHINESE 'LOWESTOFT'. Except at Worcester and Champion's Bristol, little was decorated at English factories until the 19th century, when creamware sets were so decorated by Wedgwood and Leeds, and porcelain sets by Flight & Barr, Chamberlain, Derby (fig. 7) etc.

7 ARMORIAL CHINA
Derby dish made for the
Duke of Hamilton

26

8 ART NOUVEAU Royal
Lancastrian vase by
Gordon Forsyth, 1912
(*Sotheby's Belgravia*)

9 APOSTLE JUG White
stoneware jug by Meigh,
1848 (*Victoria and
Albert Museum*)

10 ART DECO Wares designed for A. J. Wilkinson
Ltd. by Clarice Cliff, *c.* 1932 (*Geoffrey Godden*)

Art Deco (1920s and 1930s) A style evolved in the Jazz Age, partly in reaction to ART NOUVEAU, influenced by the severe functionalism of the German Bauhaus school and characterized by crisp lines, strong colour, highly stylized flowers and themes from nature (e.g. rising sun, lightning, rainbow). It also absorbed motifs from current discoveries (Tutankhamen's tomb, Aztec ruins and the Diaghilev ballet). In ceramics the functional side was typified by the cubic teapot with recessed handle, lid and spout—unbreakable and easily stacked—with matching teacups on square saucers. A lighter note is struck by a pottery figure of a cloche-hatted girl dancing, recalling memories of *thés dansants* and *The Boy Friend*. See fig. 10. (For *art décoratif*.)

Art Nouveau (1890–1910) A *fin-de-siècle* style evolved in reaction against the uglinesses of the Industrial Age, characterized by sinuous designs derived from plant life and by a love of extravagant detail for its own sake. It drew inspiration through William Morris's arts and crafts movement from Japanese designs and the Pre-Raphaelites.

More prominent on the Continent and deriving its name from a Paris shop, L'Art nouveau (1895), its chief manifestations were in architecture, illustration (Beardsley; Mucha's theatrical posters), glass (Lalique, Gallé, Tiffany), fabrics (Liberty & Co. of Regent Street); ceramic examples of the style are found on William De Morgan, Doulton and Martinware vases and Royal Lancastrian lustreware (fig. 8).

Astbury ware (c. 1720–50) A convenient label for two classes of Staffordshire lead-glazed earthenware, made by John Astbury (c. 1689–1743) of Shelton and

11 ASTBURY WARE
Earthenware figure of a
musician

by others. Many innovations (see SALTGLAZE) have
been tentatively attributed to this member of the large
Astbury family.

   1   Redware teapots, jars and other tableware,
decorated with applied reliefs. The body was fired
before glazing, given a transparent cream-coloured
glaze and refired, the result being a warm brown
colour.

   2   Figurines, in the same style as those made in
saltglaze, but using clays of two colours (red or brown
and white). They include musicians (fig. 11), horsemen, soldiers, milkmaids and some animals and birds.
(See next entry.)

Astbury-Whieldon ware (*c.* 1740–50) A convenient label for ASTBURY-type figurines in which the
transparent glaze is replaced by glazes stained green,
brown, purple, blue or black by various metallic

oxides, usually in mottled or 'tortoiseshell' mixtures; the clay was either white or a combination of white and brown. They were made by many Staffordshire potters including, according to tradition, Ralph Wood Senior. One innovation was a series of jugs in the form of soldiers, sailors, musicians etc. with detachable caps—precursors of the Toby jug. See WHIELDON WARE.

Barge teapot (*c.* 1880–1910) A vast brown-glazed teapot recognizable particularly by its having a miniature replica of itself as a lid knob (fig. 12). Coloured applied decoration (birds, flowers etc.) added a final touch of the bizarre to these wares, made chiefly in the Derby–Burton-on-Trent area and especially favoured by bargees' wives. There were also jugs and bottles in similar style.

Baroque, Rococo, Neo-Classical The first of these art-styles is of minor importance in English ceramic history. Emanating from Roman Catholic southern

12 BARGE TEAPOT
South Staffordshire,
c. 1880 (*City Museum, Stoke-on-Trent*)

Europe and watered down in the (pre-Sèvres) France of Louis XIV (1643–1715), Baroque in ceramic terms chiefly spells symmetry and strong colours (red, black, gold).

The more frivolous Rococo style, by contrast, was manifested in asymmetry, feminine colours (rose-pink, mauve, pale yellow), and wild curvaceousness seen e.g. in the elaborate scrolled bases of Bow figures (1760); see also fig. 13. Rococo is associated with the France of Louis XV (1715–74) and Sèvres (moved from Vincennes 1756), and came to England (via Meissen at first) about the time when the earliest porcelain factories began (i.e. 1745).

Very soon, however, the very different Neo-Classical influence also appeared, derived from discoveries made at Pompeii and neighbouring Herculaneum from 1748. At first these finds were thought to be Etruscan art (hence Wedgwood's 'Etruria' factory), but in fact they were Roman and Graeco-Roman. In 1758 the architect Robert Adam brought from Italy the ideas typically embodied in his austere classical fireplaces, with their swags or festoons, urns etc. In English ceramics the Neo-Classical fashion coincided with the Chelsea-Derby period (1770), and Wedgwood at Etruria (1769) found it most suitable for his un-glazed stonewares, with classical reliefs, modelled by Flaxman among others, and the Adam-style motifs and shapes. A further development was the heavier Regency style (roughly 1790–1830; corresponding to the French 'Empire' style) in which Egyptian and other exotic inspirations were added to close copies of Ancient Greece and Rome. There was also a *Revived Rococo* fashion (c. 1810), typified by the Rockingham shapes of 1826–42.

Barum ware Slipware still made at Barnstaple, Devon (Latin name Barum); it became popular when Queen Victoria bought some from Liberty & Co. in London. It may be in SGRAFFITO decoration on white over brown, or in coloured slipware, or in high relief. Pottery has been made in Barnstaple since the 13th century.

Bellarmines Globular, handled ale-bottles in brown saltglaze stoneware; on the narrow neck is the mask of a bearded man. They were so named to deride the Italian Jesuit and future Cardinal, Bellarmine, whose theological teachings at Louvain University (1569–76) gravely upset Protestant Netherlanders, but they descended in fact from a long line of masked bottles. Dwight of Fulham copied them, and they are still reproduced.

Belleek ware The Belleek factory (1857), Co. Fermanagh, Northern Ireland, became famous for parian ware glazed with an iridescent lustre resembling mother-of-pearl. Characteristic was the decorative use of marine motifs such as shells, seaweed, mermaids, dolphins and coral (fig. 14). Products included eggshell-thin tea services and openwork baskets with extremely fine flower incrustation made possible by the strength of the parian body, as well as ironstone china and earthenware. Factory still in production.

Billingsley, William (1760–1828) Porcelain decorator, famous for his roses; he introduced a naturalistic style of flower painting, using a heavily loaded brush and then wiping out the highlights. His roses were typically kidney-shaped and tightly bunched. Apprenticed to Derby, he partnered Coke at Pinxton and worked at Worcester (1808) before founding

13 BAROQUE, ROCOCO, NEO-CLASSICAL Worcester 'Gardener' with Rococo base, 1769–71 (*Dyson Perrins Museum, Worcester*)

14 BELLEEK WARE Sweetmeat dish (*Sotheby's Belgravia*)

Nantgarw and joining Dillwyn at Swansea. He devoted much of his life to costly attempts to improve the quality of porcelain and eventually at Nantgarw and Swansea was able to manufacture the very white and highly translucent soft paste that won those factories renown, and the secret of which he seems to have handed on to Rose at Coalport. Nevertheless, he died poor. He often used false names to escape creditors.

Bird-whistles Pottery birds with a whistle in the tail. One attractive form is a cuckoo in glistening yellowish glaze marbled with brown, and a hole in the breast that can be 'stopped' to produce a two-note call. A Yorkshire group has children under a treeful of bird whistles. Apparently it was an old Sussex

33

custom to place a wind-operated bird-whistle on the chimney to scare hobgoblins.

Biscuit   (1) A term of Italian origin (also 'bisque') applied to a stage in production when pottery or porcelain has been fired once and is unglazed.   (2) Specifically applied to wares (usually porcelain figures) sold in an unglazed (or only very slightly glazed) state. They were made from *c.* 1750 at Vincennes (the future Sèvres) and other Continental factories, and in England at Derby from 1773.   The composition of the body (kept secret) and the firing temperature were most important in achieving the requisite matt, porous surface, ivory-tinted at first and after *c.* 1795 given a velvety feel by volatilizing a little glaze in the kiln. The absence of decoration and glaze meant that the surface had to be completely free of imperfections; consequently, the same model cost less when decorated and glazed then when issued as a biscuit figure.   Razor-sharp modelling of detail was made possible by the absence of glaze. Most of the figures copied classical or contemporary sculpture; they were modelled at Derby by Stéphan, Spängler and others (fig. 15). Bloor (1811) did not inherit the secret and his figures were poor imitations in chalky material.   Chamberlain's Worcester and Minton also made biscuit figures.

The term may be applied to the quite different PARIAN ware, the dry stonewares (e.g. BLACK BASALT) and TERRACOTTA introduced by Wedgwood, and to the pastel-coloured figures produced in quantity by Victorian potters.

Black basalt ware (*c.* 1767)   A fine black vitreous unglazed stoneware developed by Josiah WEDGWOOD I from the cruder 'Egyptian Black' made by Stafford-

15 (*above left*) BISCUIT
Derby figure of a
shepherd, by William
Coffee, *c.* 1795 (*Victoria
and Albert Museum*)

16 (*right*)   BLACK BASALT
Rousseau, probably
Wedgwood, *c.* 1780
(*City Museum,
Stoke-on-Trent*)

17 (*left*)   BLANC-DE-CHINE
Kuan-yin figure, Chelsea,
c. 1748 (*Sotheby & Co.*)

shire potters from *c.* 1700. It was ideal for the 'Etruscan' vases favoured by Wedgwood; these were often painted red or white in the Greek classical tradition. It was also used for library busts (fig. 16), figures, plaques (with historical scenes in relief), tea-sets, mugs, inkstands etc. Black basalt was copied by other potters, notably by Spode. Wedgwood preferred the Latin form of the name, black *basaltes*.

Blanc-de-chine White or near-white richly glazed porcelain of great beauty in which, in Fukien province during the Ming period, possibly in the 17th century, Buddhist figures were made, particularly of Kuan-yin, the graceful goddess of mercy (fig. 17). Other wares were made, often with applied prunus blossom in relief. Chelsea, Bow and Longton Hall made figures (including Kuan-yin), animals and sprig-decorated wares in this style.

'Blind Earl' pattern A famous Worcester coloured pattern of the 1760s, typically used on dishes, with large sprays of moulded leaves (hand-modelled) and applied buds branching from a twig that forms the handle (fig. 18). It is named after an Earl of Coventry blinded in a hunting accident; the tradition that it was created for him is disproved by the dates.

18 'BLIND EARL' PATTERN

Blue-and-white A name given to porcelain, earthernware or stoneware painted or printed under-glaze in blue. The original purpose of this development was to undercut the Chinese blue-and-white ('Old Nankin') which flooded the 18th-century market for medium-price domestic wares—and pseudo-Chinese designs were commonest at first. The glaze protected patterns from damage by knife, fork or spoon, and cobalt blue was, at first, the only colour that could be relied on to withstand the temperature required in glazing.

Blue-painted wares were produced by all 18th-century English porcelain factories (although Chelsea examples are rare). All except Chelsea also adopted blue TRANSFER-PRINTING, especially Worcester, Caughley (in violet-blue) and Lowestoft. Thomas Turner founded Caughley (1774) primarily to produce blue-and-white transfer-printed porcelain tableware.

Staffordshire potters were slow to take up even painted underglaze blue; a painted creamware bowl by Booth, dated 1743, seems to have been experimental. The best-selling 'Staffordshire blue' owes its existence to Spode, who from 1781 applied printed blue patterns successively to his creamware, pearlware, bone china and stone china with such success that Davenport, Wedgwood and eventually hundreds of Staffordshire potters followed his example (fig. 19); blue-and-white was soon being made also in Liverpool, Leeds, Swansea and other centres, but as most of it was unmarked early examples tend to be lumped together as 'Staffordshire blue'. Patterns were freely pirated and attribution of unmarked pieces is virtually impossible.

The heyday of Staffordshire blue was 1815–40,

19 (*left*) BLUE-AND-WHITE Staffordshire plate with octagonal *chinoiserie* design, c. 1810–25 (*Mary Payton Antiques*)

20 (*right*) BLUE-AND-WHITE Staffordshire octagonal dish with North Carolina scene, early 19th century (*City Museum, Stoke-on-Trent*)

when a lucrative trade was built up with the U.S.A., especially in wares printed with American scenes (fig. 20). To CHINOISERIES, e.g. the WILLOW PATTERN and the Caughley 'Fisherman' pattern (c. 1790), were added, from c. 1805, designs such as those mentioned under SPODE. Early Staffordshire blue earthenware should be light in weight, have a bluish glaze, present a slightly rippled surface when viewed at an angle, and the flatware should (usually) have three stilt-marks near the rim, above or below the surface. The best of it (c. 1806–30) has been copied and artificially 'aged', but the fakes lack these characteristics.

Bocage The background of stylized leaves and flowers given to some porcelain and pottery figures and groups. In the early days of porcelain there had always to be some device to prop up a figure (otherwise it would collapse in the kiln). From the usual tree-trunk support Meissen developed the light bocage (French for 'grove', 'copse') which Bow, Chelsea and, later, Derby turned into an elaborate arbour-like background, used on pieces designed for the cabinet and therefore to be viewed from the front only. In pottery the WALTON SCHOOL made distinctive use of bocages. (Plate 1; fig. 13.)

Booth of Tunstall A name which goes back to the 18th century, but this pottery is best known for its excellent reproductions in earthenware of 18th-century Worcester and other porcelain, especially blue-and-white plates, made in this century. The original marks were also copied, combined with a 'B'.

Boots and shoes Pottery and porcelain examples range from a Bristol delftware pair of court shoes with a floral pattern in blue (1729) to a Turkish slipper (Minton) and the many hand-painted Victorian and Edwardian bone-china containers or flower-holders of various kinds.

Boot-warmer An astonishing mid-Victorian item, shaped like a boot, filled with hot water and placed inside a boot to warm it. They are found in 'Rockingham'-glazed pottery (and also in glass).

Bow (*c.* 1746–76)   Bow, in what is now east London, started as a workshop where an Irish portraitist, Thomas Frye, with others experimented on various ingredients to find a porcelain competitive with Chinese imports.   If its existence is dated from his first patent (December 1744), Bow preceded Chelsea, but there is no evidence of commercial production till 1746/47 and the factory did not really get going until after Frye's second patent (November 1749) covering the first bone-ash china (see Introduction, page 16).

Bow remained innovatory to the end; its vast output varied greatly in quality and appearance, making identification at times difficult, the only constants being the high bone-ash ('phosphatic') content and the presence of a special white clay imported from South Carolina. The glaze, laid on thickly, varying from greyish to bluish, reached its best in a soft creamy colour (*c.* 1750); some is too easily scratched.   The porcelain, thickly potted, was heavy, not very translucent, and often developed internal cracks.

Founded at the peak of the CHINOISERIE vogue (and hence called the New Canton factory), Bow at first copied its designs directly from Chinese and Japanese wares.   It concentrated consistently on durable tablewares which undercut Chelsea's in price; from 1750, figures became the other mainstay.   During the first decade tableware was white, with applied white sprigs, or blurred, and at first very pale, blue-and-white; tea-sets were a speciality.   From *c.* 1753 enamelled wares were added to the range.   Octagonal plates and bell-shaped mugs (see dust-jacket) were especially typical of Bow.

The early figures, possibly all by the 'Muses Modeller' (1750–54; so called from a set of Muses in his style), are mostly on plain bases and designed to be left white—hence an exaggeration of the eyebrows, open mouth and garment folds which are his hallmarks; they included actors in popular roles (Garrick, Peg Woffington etc.). In general Bow went its own way and many of its figures break with the mainstream Meissen-Chelsea tradition of courtly sophistication. From c. 1754, bases evolved from plain to increasingly rococo styles and finally the elaborately scrolled four-footed base with frontal swag typical from c. 1760 to the end, the later Neo-Classical vogue being ignored; this adherence to the rococo long after it had become unfashionable may have contributed to Bow's downfall. The figures themselves were increasingly boldly, even garishly, coloured. Square holes at the back of the base for metal accessories (flower-holders, candle sockets) are a Bow feature from 1755.

The later 1750s saw more ornate wares, e.g. fine sets of underglaze-blue vases with well painted highly exotic birds in the reserves; partridge tureens; animal and bird figures (dogs, hares, owls, hens); England's first transfer-printed wares, by Hancock (1756; see Introduction, page 20); Meissen-style sprigs and insects; and the typical Kakiemon quail pattern. Some of these developments are attributed to an influx of Chelsea artists at the close of its Red Anchor period.

Frye retired in 1759, but his patented monopoly of phosphatic porcelain and liquid lead glaze did not expire until 1763, though possibly shared under licence with Chelsea. As elsewhere, more elaboration and more gilding marked a general decline in taste, though some excellent pieces were still made, e.g. plates painted with Fragonard or Boucher themes; much seems to have been decorated elsewhere, in a palette in which light blue and crimson predominated. The factory was probably bought by William Duesbury of Derby.

Bristol   See CHAMPION'S BRISTOL; LUND'S BRISTOL.

Brownware   Salt-glazed brown stoneware of the kind made since the 17th century in Nottingham, Derbyshire, London and elsewhere. The colour might be brown, buff or chocolate, and the decoration carved or with impressed designs. Brownware was used in making countless POSSET-POTS, LOVING CUPS, Toby jugs, candlesticks, figures and the wares mentioned under STONEWARE and NOTTINGHAM WARE. A favourite form was the *hunting jug* (and the similar mugs) bearing well-executed hunting scenes carved in deep relief, with greyhound handles (fig. 22); some were made at Isleworth, Middlesex, in the early 19th century.

Buttons   Porcelain buttons were made in the first half of the 19th century, mostly mass-produced, moulded and enamelled in specially strengthened ironstone-type china.

Cadogan teapot   A lidless teapot filled through a hole in the base which was the end of a spiral tube reaching to near the top of the pot; the principle was that of the well inkpot (fig. 21). It was so called after the Hon. Mrs Cadogan who commissioned (*c*. 1790) the Rockingham pottery to make a teapot in imitation of a Chinese peach-shaped wine-pot she admired. Cadogans became a vogue (when the Prince Regent started drinking *wine* from them) and were also made by Davenport, Copeland and others, often with the characteristic Rockingham purplish-brown glaze.

21 (*top*) CADOGAN TEAPOT
Copeland & Garrett specimen,
c. 1820 (*Spode-Copeland
Museum*)

22 (*left*) BROWNWARE
Copeland & Garrett hunting
jug. *c.* 1830s (*Spode-
Copeland Museum*)

23 (*right*) CANDLESNUFFERS
'Mr Caudle', Royal Worcester,
c. 1880 (*Mary Payton
Antiques*)

Candlesnuffers Small hollow porcelain figures, first made as detachable parts of an elaborate candle-stick, later separately with or without a stand; made by Minton, Derby, Royal Worcester (fig. 23). Favourite forms were Jenny Lind (with a nightingale's head), Winter, nuns, owls etc.

Candlesticks Bow, Chelsea and Derby made some very elaborate candlesticks with figures holding up flower-shaped sockets, the sepals forming the neces-sary grease-pans. Others might be shaped much like silver models, but flower-encrusted, and there were some very austere Neo-Classical models in creamware. Bow figures might have sockets to take branched metal candelabra. The chief uses were for the dining-table, dressing-table and desk.

The chamber-candlestick, to light the way to bed, could also be a very delicate concoction of flower encrustation (fig. 24). The taperstick was shorter, with a narrow socket, and could be used at the desk for sealing letters, or brought in with the tea-things, partly to give light but mainly for its perfumed bees-wax.

Cane and Bamboo ware (*c.* 1785) Wedgwood's tan-coloured unglazed stoneware, usually decorated in relief and sometimes further embellished with touches of blue, green or red. Wares shaped and coloured so as to look as if made of sections of bamboo were called Bamboo ware (fig. 25). Tea-sets, jugs, pot-pourri bowls, bulb-pots, candlesticks etc. were made in these wares; also 'pie-crust' covers and dishes, made to imitate the real thing when flour was taxed during the Napoleonic Wars.

25 CANE AND BAMBOO WARE Copeland & Garrett Bamboo-ware teapot. *c.* 1795 (*Spode-Copeland Museum*)

26 CASTLEFORD Moulded teapot. *c.* 1800–20 (*Victoria and Albert Museum*)

Carpet balls   Stoneware or earthenware balls for an early Victorian game of bowls played preferably in a carpeted corridor.   A full set consisted of one plain ball and six with coloured rings or other patterns.

Castleford (*c.* 1790–1820)   A south Yorkshire factory near Leeds, founded by David Dunderdale who had been apprenticed at Leeds Pottery; best known for its fine white scantily glazed stoneware teapots with panels outlined in blue (sometimes red), and moulded classical reliefs (fig. 26).   Very few are marked, and similar teapots, some marked '22', were made by other (perhaps Staffordshire) potters.   In general the four narrow corner panels are concave in true Castleford, convex (bulging) in the others—but there seem to be exceptions.   The lids may be sliding or hinged.

Castleford, however, produced much else: other teaware in the same thin semi-translucent felspathic stoneware; good creamware, much of it exported; transfer-printed earthenware in blue or brown; some inferior BLACK BASALT; large jugs with a wide dark brown collar and classical reliefs.   As so little is marked, 'Castleford' is more a generic than a specific name.

Castle Hedingham (*c.* 1870–1905)   An Essex art pottery making fantastically designed teapots, urns, 'Essex jugs' etc. in pottery which chipped easily. The mark is a castle with the initials of the artist, Edward Bingham.   See fig 27.

Caughley (1775–99)   A Shropshire porcelain factory (pronounced calf'ly) established near Broseley and Coalport by Thomas Turner; its wares are sometimes called (and marked) 'Salopian'.   Turner had

learnt engraving at Worcester under Robert Hancock, who joined him at Caughley. The new factory used the same soapstone body as Worcester (Davis/Flight period), and copied many of their printed patterns; resemblances were so close that only recently has it been shown that much 'Caughley' was made at Worcester. The tradition that porcelain from the main Worcester factory was decorated at Caughley seems unfounded; but much Caughley was sold to, and some decorated by, the separate firm, Chamberlain's Worcester. In fact Turner tried to undersell Davis/Flight in blue-printed useful wares, which formed the bulk of Caughley's output.

Many patterns are Chinese-style landscapes (fig. 28), but those marked with disguised Chinese numerals are now thought to be Worcester. Some of the designs used by both factories are distinguishable by differences in detail, e.g. the fishing-line in the 'Fisherman' pattern is taut on Caughley, slack on Worcester; shading was by parallel lines at Caughley, cross-hatched or hand-washed at Worcester; the familiar cabbage-leaf mask-jugs have the eyes of the face-mask open on Caughley, closed on Worcester (see fig. 62); the filled-in or shaded crescent mark is usually (perhaps always) Worcester, the open version may be Caughley or Coalport. Gilding is found on Chinese-style printed designs and underglaze blue-painted European landscapes or floral sprays; most overglaze enamel and gilt decoration seems to be the work of Chamberlain or London decorators. A print of the world's first iron bridge (1779) at neighbouring Coalbrookdale is found on Caughley and Coalport.

Defeated by competition from bone china and Staffordshire blue, Turner sold the factory to his former apprentice, John Rose (see COALPORT). Possibly during Turner's last few years, and certainly under Rose, hard-paste porcelain was made at Caughley and is provisionally termed Caughley/Coalport hard-paste. New Hall shapes and patterns (and even pattern numbers) were closely copied in this body.

Chamberlain's Worcester (c. 1786–1852) A breakaway firm founded on the site of the present Royal Worcester Co. by Robert Chamberlain, after Flight bought the main Worcester factory; Chamber-

29 CHAMBERLAIN'S
WORCESTER Vase
c. 1840 (*Victoria and
Albert Museum*)

lain had been Dr Wall's first apprentice. At first it decorated wares bought, usually in the white, from Caughley and some from Flight. In 1791 Chamberlain began making his own porcelain, not very successfully initially, but so greatly improved by 1800 as to constitute a threat to the parent firm, which was absorbed in 1840 (and styled 'Chamberlain & Co.') the better to meet rivalry from Staffordshire bone china. Wares were in many ways similar to those of FLIGHT & BARR, if sometimes over-ornate (fig. 29). Baxter decorated for both, and several Flight artists joined Chamberlain, whose son also painted some pieces. In addition a very fine porcelain ('Regent china') was developed in 1811, but proved too costly.

From 1840 there were financial troubles and unsuccessful experiments which led to the management being taken over by *Kerr & Binns* (1852–62). New artists and ideas were introduced, e.g. Renaissance pictures painted in white enamel on deep blue grounds ('Limoges enamels'), which suited contemporary taste. Kerr retired and Binns was left to form a new company, parent of today's ROYAL WORCESTER PORCELAIN CO.

Champion's Bristol (1773–81)

PLYMOUTH hard-paste production was continued at Bristol until Cookworthy handed over management and sold his patent to one of the original Plymouth shareholders, Richard Champion, a shrewder businessman and a fellow Quaker. A complete change in style (to 'near-Dresden') is indicated in a November 1772 advertisement; the hard paste was improved, better artists were employed, and Sèvres-style Neo-Classical decoration replaced rococo. Champion concentrated chiefly on tea and coffee sets, including some expensive commissioned armorial services but also cheaper 'cottage china'. More figures were made, decorated with Quaker simplicity, but these are generally regarded as rather coarsely modelled and stiff. A Champion speciality was miniature oval biscuit plaques, modelled in relief with armorial bearings, portraits, flowers or classical figures, framed and sold or given to influential friends.

Champion's high ambitions were partly based on the potentialities of a market in the American colonies; the Revolution and the capture of his ships by the French were severe blows and, together with costly litigation over the extension of his patent (opposed by Wedgwood) and competition from newcomers such as Caughley in addition to older rivals such as Worcester and Derby, led to heavy losses. Champion therefore sold his patent to the group of Staffordshire potters who founded New Hall.

Chelsea (c. 1745–70) It is uncertain whether Chelsea or Bow was the earliest English porcelain factory; Chelsea is more highly esteemed and offered a wider range, but quality varied. Founded by a Flemish silversmith, Nicholas Sprimont, managed at first by a French jeweller, and relying heavily for its figures on another Fleming, Joseph Willems, Chelsea alone aimed at the luxury market tapped by Meissen and Sèvres, usually imitating the former until Sèvres became dominant in the Gold Anchor period. By contrast Bow was chiefly influenced by Chinese models.

The marks used divide Chelsea into brief but indeterminate periods: Triangle (to 1749), Raised Anchor (to 1752), Red Anchor (to 1756, followed by a break in production), Gold Anchor (1758/9–70) and finally CHELSEA-DERBY. It is said that genuine Chelsea is outnumbered by reproductions (e.g. Coalport, Minton) and fakes (especially Samsons with oversize gold anchors). Tablewares, contrary to general belief, predominated; very little blue-and-white was made.

The first paste was a milk-white, highly translucent glassy frit, with a soft glaze now yellowed with age; it was prone to warping and crazing, and 'pinholes' are characteristic. Triangle products (almost all are in museums) were mostly tea and coffee sets, with moulded decoration or 'raised' flowers; painted sprigs and insects often concealed defects. The earliest (and most faked) piece is the Goat and Bee jug, copied from a silver model.

The typical Raised Anchor body was less glassy, slightly greyish and had an opaque look due to tin in a glaze so thick that it formed pools; the pinholes enlarged to become 'moons'. The stronger paste permitted figures to be made for the first time; enamelled birds are especially attractive.

Red Anchor wares are most prized; the finer the ware the smaller the anchor, often difficult to spot. Translucency was high; moons continued; crazing was conquered for a time but returned; spur marks are found under plates, as in the next period. Characteristic products are sparsely decorated moulded plates and leaf-shaped dishes; tureens in the form of hen and chickens, other birds, animals, fish or vegetables; a wide range of figures, e.g. COMMEDIA DELL' ARTE (fig. 35), peasants and the best Chelsea Classical figures—some to be used as flower-holders, candlesticks or sweetmeat stands. Sprimont, who may have bought the GIRL-IN-A-SWING FACTORY, continued the making of their scent-bottles and other Chelsea toys. Decoration included 'Hans Sloane' copies of botanical plates, some excellent Aesop's fable themes by O'Neale, exotic birds, Meissen landscapes and JAPAN PATTERNS.

The Gold Anchor period was characterized by Sèvres rococo styles; increasingly elaborate form and decoration, especially mercury gilding; and richly coloured grounds, notably turquoise, claret and several blues. BOCAGES were introduced; figures in general are inferior to Red Anchor examples. Wares were thickly potted in a chalky-white bone-ash paste; moons disappeared but crazing returned; a glassier glaze formed greenish pools.

Chelsea-Derby (1770–84) The name properly applied to wares made at Chelsea, after Duesbury of

Derby bought Sprimont's Chelsea factory. Unfortunately no one is sure which those wares are, even those with a combined mark (anchor and crown; anchor and D, which might stand for Derby or Duesbury). Various mutually contradictory criteria have been suggested, but it appears that the factories exchanged both raw materials and undecorated pieces, making confusion worse confounded.

It seems likely that Chelsea-Derby was characterized by a thinly potted bone-ash body and craze-free glaze, both an improvement on Gold Anchor. Restraint in style (except gilding) was restored with the coming of Neo-Classical fashions. Fine Sèvres-type tablewares were made, with good but cheaper red or blue grounds; also much blue-and-white. Figures (fig. 50) were greatly influenced in style by Derby. The Chelsea factory was closed in 1784 and the moulds sent to Derby.

Chessmen Wedgwood issued several sets modelled by Flaxman in jasper, the figures being characters from *Macbeth*, *Hamlet* etc. They were made in quantity from 1784, and later copied by Samson. Stoneware sets, with George III as the King and Scots Guards as pawns, are attributed to Castleford. Meissen sets were imitated by Rockingham, substituting Tudor costume. Minton made parian sets and Doulton made chessmen which, since they were modelled by George Tinworth, were turned into his favourite mice. See fig. 31; also MARTINWARE.

Children's plates Small earthenware plates, some octagonal, with transfer-printed scenes (usually black-and-white), embossed borders (usually coloured) and a title or text. Some subjects were purely decorative (birds, flowers, children's games), others educational (alphabet borders, Biblical scenes, pious texts, nursery rhymes).

These plates were made mostly between 1830 and 1850 in Swansea (typically with an embossed daisy border), Staffordshire, Sunderland and Scotland. See fig. 30.

Chinese 'Lowestoft' An old name for 18th-century Chinese hard-paste export table services, once mistakenly thought to hail from Lowestoft. Some resembled Lowestoft in decoration, whether blue-and-

30 (*right*) CHILDREN'S PLATES 'Uncle Tom'. *c.* 1840 (*Mary Payton Antiques*)

31 (*below left*) CHESSMEN Queen from pottery set in Prattware colours

32 (*below right*) CHINESE 'LOWESTOFT' (*Mary Payton Antiques*)

white or polychrome, though it is difficult to determine who was copying whom (fig. 32). Vast quantities were shipped to Europe and, although the myth that they had any connection with Lowestoft was exploded long ago, some is still displayed as 'Lowestoft'. Chinese-decorated ARMORIAL CHINA is also still mis-called 'Armorial Lowestoft'.

Chinoiserie The vogue for all things Chinese reached England c. 1740, leading to Chinese Chippendale and lacquer furniture. In ceramics it had reached Meissen and French porcelain centres c. 1725 and came to Chelsea, Bow (which called itself 'New Canton') and Worcester (the 'Tonquin' Co.) via Sèvres; other sources were Dutch delftware (an influence dominant in blue-and-white), the *chinoiserie* paintings of Watteau and Boucher, among others, and travel-book engravings. Direct copying from Chinese originals began c. 1760, but the English always preferred a fanciful WILLOW PATTERN land to anything remotely like the real thing, and even the Chinese potters indulged them.

Chinoiserie features ranged from LONG ELIZAS to particular flowers (chrysanthemum, prunus, paeony). Especially striking among polychrome designs are the Ho-ho bird, said to be the phoenix; the hermaphrodite Kylin with dragon head and not very deer-like scaly body; and the Dog of Fo, a temple guard-dog breathing out fire in all directions through its fearsome teeth. New Hall ran a special line in moon-faced mandarins resembling wooden toys, loitering (without discernible intent) about garden or courtyard. Blue-and-white designs abounded with Willow Pattern features plus unexpected garden fauna such as elephant, giraffe, camel and weird birds.

The taste for *chinoiserie* succumbed on the Continent before the Neo-Classical onslaught, but in England it has lingered on, increasingly mixed up with *japonaiserie* (see JAPAN PATTERNS and Plate 2).

Chocolate sets 'Jocalatte', as Pepys called it, was at first more popular than tea, and was drunk at breakfast or in coffee houses. Chocolate pots were generally smaller than coffee pots and followed the silver shape in having the handle at right-angles to the spout (a feature later transferred to coffee pots). The cups were very elaborate, resembling caudle cups (see POSSET POTS AND CAUDLE CUPS).

Clobbered A derogatory adjective for blue-and-white underglaze-painted wares which a faker has tried to make look richer, and therefore pricier, by adding enamel colours, usually in execrable taste in reds, greens, yellows and gilding. The practice goes back to the early 19th century.

Coalbrookdale (1) A synonym for 19th-century flower-encrusted bone china (*c.* 1820–60), a 'revived rococo' fashion inspired by the 18th-century ornamental pieces made in this style by Longton Hall, Chelsea, Derby, Bow and Worcester. In the best specimens each applied flower has individually moulded and naturalistically coloured paper-thin petals and leaves; there was a later descent to mass-moulded work. A great range of flowers was copied, from tiny forget-me-nots to inch-wide roses. Favourite wares were scent bottles, pierced-edge baskets with fruit and flowers in full relief (fig. 79), potpourris, pastille-burners, candlesticks, trays, spill and other vases (Plate 3; fig. 58).

They were made by Rockingham, Coalport (marked 'C Dale', 'C.D.' etc.), Bloor Derby, Grainger's Worcester, Davenport and Copeland, but it has recently been discovered that some, perhaps most, of the best were made by Minton, many given a pseudo-Dresden mark.

(2) The name, at first spelt Colebrook Dale, given to the Coalport factory in 1828; it was near Coalbrookdale (north of Much Wenlock, Shropshire), which is interesting in itself as being the cradle of the Industrial Revolution. After the discovery there of coal and iron in the 18th century, coal began to replace charcoal in the smelting of iron. The deep Severn gorge near by was spanned by the world's first iron bridge, built by Abraham Darby (1779) and still standing. Today Wenlock borough includes Coalbrookdale, Broseley, Ironbridge and MADELEY—all names with ceramic associations.

Coalport (c. 1796–today) A Shropshire factory founded by John Rose when he left Caughley; it was sited on the east bank of the Severn opposite Caughley (which Rose bought up in 1799 and demolished in 1814). In this period some hard-paste porcelain was made (see CAUGHLEY). There is a tradition that in 1820 Rose ended competition from Nantgarw and Swansea by buying their equipment and moulds and engaging Billingsley and Walker to come to Coalport. An 1860s factory mark incorporated the initials C, N, S, standing for these three factories, but there remains considerable doubt about the terms of any agreement with the two latter. The last of the Rose family retired in 1862, and the firm moved in 1926 to Stoke, Staffordshire.

Coalport's best period opened in 1820 with the introduction of a brilliantly white and very translucent hard felspar china and a new leadless glaze (also felspathic). Thereafter the factory became, as it remains, famous for high-quality tablewares with distinctive ground colours, e.g. maroon, *gros bleu*, several greens, the Sèvres *rose pompadour* (or ·*rose dubarry*; less flatteringly, 'blancmange pink') and a dark underglaze blue. Also notable were ornamental wares made to suit the revived fashion for rococo (1820–40), including flower-encrusted COALBROOK-DALE pieces; Parian figures (1850s); and copies (some with faked marks) of Chelsea (including the Goat and Bee jug), Meissen and, from 1840, Sèvres—the latter so good that Rose bought one at auction, thinking it genuine. See Plate 3.

Cockle plates Small plates for cockles, whelks or eels, many made in Sunderland or Swansea (fig. 33) and transfer-printed with seaside views, shells, anchors etc. Some bear the arms of the Oddfellows or other friendly societies and were used at their formal high teas.

Comfit-holders Pairs of figures holding small baskets, bowls or shells in which were placed tiny sugared breath-sweeteners—Shakespeare's 'kissing-

33 COCKLE PLATES
Swansea example
(*National Museum of Wales*)

34 COMFIT-HOLDER
Derby, c. 1765

35 COMMEDIA DELL'
ARTE Chelsea Red Anchor
figure of Scapin (*Christie's*)

comfits'—for use after drinking, smoking, or eating
the far-from-fresh meats of winter, and/or before
kissing. Made of aniseed, celery, coriander, caraway
etc., these comfits ('confections') were thus the precursors of today's chlorophyll cachous. The comfit-
holders—traditional shepherdesses, Turks, gardeners
etc.—were part of the elaborate decoration of the
18th-century dessert table at informal parties. They
were made well on into the latter half of the 19th
century by most of the leading porcelain factories
(fig. 34).

Commedia dell' arte Some early English porcelain
figures are derived from the stock figures in this form
of theatrical entertainment, which spread over Europe

from Italy (where it originated in the 16th century). Masked actors ad-libbed their way through a traditional story of an elopement. The be-spectacled and be-slippered Pantaloon tries to make his daughter Columbine marry 'The Captain', son of 'The Doctor'; but she loves Harlequin. Many servants join in the consequent intrigues, among them Pierrot, Punch and the cowardly braggart soldier, Scaramouche.

Kändler (at Meissen) and Bustelli (Nymphenburg) made some outstanding *commedia dell' arte* figures, which inspired those of Bow, Chelsea (fig. 35) and Derby. (Abbreviated from the Italian for 'A comedy improvised by the actors' profession (*arte*)'.)

Commemorative china Strictly, this term is confined to pieces which commemorate an event within a short time after its occurrence; this definition rules out, e.g. Waterloo replicas issued at Wellington's death, most Napoleonic subjects and many Nelson jugs, as well as recent limited-edition issues commemorating centenaries etc.

Commemorative china became popular *c.* 1780 after the introduction of transfer printing and cheaply produced creamware. Main categories are: Royal births (fig. 36), weddings, coronations, jubilees and deaths; great victories; disasters (often sold to raise funds for relief); political campaigns (Reform, 1832; Free Trade, 1840), electioneering and, occasionally, satire. The usual forms are mugs, jugs, plates, teapots and teacups, transfer-printed often in black, sometimes on lustreware or early Prattware.

Much was generated by misguided public (and malicious Whig) support for George IV's wife Caroline, whom he barred from his coronation (1821) after evidence of her adulteries had been presented to the

36 COMMEMORATIVE CHINA 'Souvenir of Princess Elizabeth', one item from a tea-set (*Mary Payton Antiques*)

37 (*above right*) COMMEMORATIVE CHINA Queen Caroline jug; note the reference to the 'Green-Bag crew' (*J. & J. May*)

38 COMMEMORATIVE CHINA Russian bear hugging Napoleon (*Willett Collection, Brighton*)

House of Lords, in a much-mentioned green bag (fig. 37); also by the popularity of the fruit of their single and singular union, Princess Charlotte, who married Leopold of Belgium and died young. Coronation mugs for Queen Victoria are now very rare; after Prince Albert's death (1861) she became a recluse and few royal commemorative pieces were issued until the Golden Jubilee (1887). See CRICKET THEMES; RAILWAY THEMES.

As indicated, most of the many pieces depicting Napoleon as a Corsican monkey capering about the Channel coast and garrulously gibbering in a fantastic pidgin English, are not truly commemorative; sad to confess, they were not made until Napoleon was safe on St Helena. See also fig. 38.

Copeland (& Garrett) See SPODE.

Cornucopia A horn of plenty, usually flat-backed to hang on a wall, made in many kinds of pottery and porcelain; fashionable *c.* 1750–1870, they were used for flowers or ivy. Some have moulded bird or floral decoration (fig. 39), others are in blue-and-white.

The origin of the shape lies in Greek mythology. The infant Zeus, kept alive by a Cretan princess with

39 CORNUCOPIA
Worcester, First Period

goat's milk, in gratitude (not to the goat) broke off one of its horns and gave it to the princess, promising that it would always be filled with whatever its possessor wished.

Cottages A convenient term covering china cottages, castles, toll-houses or churches, often made to burn pastilles emitting pungent smoke through the chimney—a useful function when sanitation was primitive (Plate 6). These may have lift-off roofs, and gables, dormer windows, occasionally human figures or a dog. Some were night-light holders whose cut-out windows gleamed comfortingly in children's bedrooms. Money-boxes, broken to retrieve the pennies, are rarer.

Some were in early Prattware; the better porcelain examples of 1820–40 are usually called 'Rockingham' but are not mentioned in that factory's records; Coalport, Minton, Worcester and Derby made them, and many are in Staffordshire bone china. Later, cruder pottery models came from Staffordshire, Yorkshire and Scotland.

Cow-creamer (18th–19th centuries) A milk jug modelled in the form of a cow, with curved tail as handle, mouth as spout and detachable 'saddle' on the back as lid. They were made in every kind of ware and colour by many potters.

Most survivors are from Staffordshire or Swansea, the former often with black or brown markings, some in lustre. Identification is difficult, but Staffordshire characteristics possibly include a tail curving on to the back, oval green base with a large moulded daisy, and an added milkmaid figure. Early specimens had thin flat rectangular bases. Swansea models (Plate 8) were often transfer-printed, had a rectangular moulded base and the tail curving to the flank.

After *c.* 1850 cow-creamers were made for decoration rather than use since, being impossible to clean properly, they were unhygienic.

Cradles Miniature pottery imitations of wicker basket cradles made as christening presents *c.* 1700–1850. The earliest, 4–12 in. (100–300 mm) long, were in slipware (fig. 40) and might contain a crudely hand-modelled baby; a few were dated. Later cradles were moulded in saltglaze or other stoneware or in earthenware; decoration might be tortoiseshell, the Wedgwood green glaze, or bright painted colours. Some are fitted as pincushions.

Creamware (*c.* 1720–today) Lightweight thinly potted lead-glazed cream-coloured earthenware, made with the same ingredients as the SALTGLAZE body but fired at a lower temperature. Its invention is attributed to one of the Astburys and to Enoch Booth, the latter responsible (*c.* 1740) for the characteristic butter-coloured fluid glaze (of ground lead, flint and pipeclay) in which the wares were dipped. In the late 18th century it displaced saltglaze and delftware as the staple earthenware product, and was exported in very great quantity. It reached perfection at LEEDS and was developed by Wedgwood (fig. 41) in the form of QUEEN'S WARE and PEARLWARE; Enoch Wood, Spode, Davenport and others in Staffordshire, Derby, Liverpool, Swansea, Bristol and elsewhere all made creamware.

Typical forms of decoration were *pierce work* (plate-rims, baskets etc. with various openwork patterns punched out by hand; a Leeds speciality); *basket work*

40 CRADLES
Staffordshire
slipware cradle,
c. 1700 (*Victoria
and Albert
Museum*)

41 CREAMWARE
Wedgwood plate,
with Kenilworth
Castle, *c.* 1774
(*City Museum,
Stoke-on-Trent*)

(openwork basket designs); intertwined handles on jugs; free-painted flowers, often in red and black or a distinctive green; teapots with crabstock handles and spouts, decorated with scenes, portraits, birds etc. in underglaze blue, transfer-printed, enamel-painted or in tortoiseshell; jugs and loving-cups with a name or dedication in elaborate scrollwork. Many pieces were left undecorated.

Cricket themes The game is ceramically depicted from at least 1820—a blue-and-white dish showing top-hatted cricketers with baseball bats—down to the heyday of Hobbs and Bradman. Flatbacks (c. 1843; fig. 42) show named cricketers (Pilch and Box) before a wicket and tree-trunk spill-holder resembling at first glance a five-handed wicket-keeper. These two celebrities and Lillywhite also appear in relief on Prattware jugs, Minton mugs and in silver lustre—the Pratt jugs reproduced at Leeds as recently as 1906. Flatbacks of helmeted Volunteer officers at the wicket in full regimentals appeared in 1859; as there was a war-scare at the time they were presumably ready to wield what look like canoe-paddles to hit either ball or Frenchman for six. Transfer-printed pieces commemorate specific matches of this period, and a Coalport mug W. G. Grace's hundredth century (1895).

Daniel family Staffordshire potters at Stoke. Henry and Richard Daniel (c. 1825–54) made stone china and high-quality porcelain notable for colour grounds (applied by a new method) and gilding. Henry had, from 1802, been chief enamel decorator at Spode, where he is said to have introduced embossed unburnished gilding.

Davenport (1793–1887) A Staffordshire firm founded at Longport by John Davenport and carried on by his sons. For the first few years only earthenware was made, including creamware and stone china; much of it was attractively decorated with underglaze blue transfer-prints, or painted landscapes. Porcelain (bone china) was first made c. 1805, until the 1830s mostly for the cheaper market, when it was greyish and sparsely decorated in the New Hall style. Then artists were engaged from Derby and elsewhere, leading to the addition of more expensive lines of fine

43 (*right*) DELFTWARE
Blue-dash charger,
possibly Bristol, in blue,
red and yellow with
portrait of Charles I
(*Christie's*)

42 (*above*) CRICKET
THEMES Staffordshire
figure, possibly of
Julius Caesar, *c.* 1865
(*Sotheby's Belgravia*)

44 DE MORGAN,
WILLIAM Vase
painted in lustre
colours, *c.* 1903
(*Victoria and
Albert Museum*)

45 DR SYNTAX
Walton/Salt-type
Staffordshire figure,
c. 1825; 'Landing at
Calais' (*City
Museum, Stoke-on-
Trent*)

white china (Plate 3), colourfully decorated, heavily gilded and with elaborate landscapes, well-painted roses and other flowers, or still-lifes etc.; an apple-green ground was particularly successful and the dessert services of the 1850–70 period are especially admired. In the last two decades 'Japan' patterns were introduced. Some authorities feel that the better quality Davenport wares are still under-valued.

Delftware (16th–18th centuries) In England the name given to tin-glazed earthenware fired at low temperature; the tin (added to lead) gave an opaque white finish on which decoration, usually in blue, yellow and green, had to be painted quickly on to the absorbent glaze, giving a characteristically spontaneous quality. The designs were sometimes of much the same type as on Toft's SLIPWARE, and quite as bizarre. One type of this ware, called '*blue-dash chargers*' (fig. 43), took the form of large shallow dishes of which the rims were decorated with dashes of blue; these were intended to be hung as WALL PLAQUES.

The origin of delftware goes back to a Mesopotamian technique brought by the Moors to Spain (*Hispano-Mauresque ware*) and thence to Italy (*maiolica*, 'from Majorca'; *faience*, 'made at Faenza') and the Low Countries (*Delft*) and brought to England (Norwich) by two Dutchmen *c.* 1571. It was made in London (Lambeth and Southwark), Bristol, Liverpool, Dublin, Glasgow and elsewhere. Too fragile to be really serviceable (surviving examples are usually chipped or broken), it was eventually displaced by CREAMWARE. See also figs. 52 and 93.

Della Robbia ware (1894–1906) Art pottery of striking, sometimes grotesque, shapes decorated with a mixture of painting and SGRAFFITO, usually with a vivid green glaze, made by the Della Robbia Pottery, Birkenhead. The name implied a revival of the opaque-glazed and enamelled terracotta made by the Della Robbia family in 15th- and 16th-century Florence. Compare 'PALISSY' WARE.

De Morgan, William (1839–1917)   The versatile inventor, novelist and potter who set up a STUDIO POTTERY in Chelsea and elsewhere in London (1872–1907).   His friendship with William Morris and Burne-Jones linked him to the Arts and Crafts movement and the Pre-Raphaelites.

He tried to revive Hispano-Mauresque iridescent lustreware (see DELFTWARE) and to recapture the shapes and colours (turquoise, other blues and greens, and red) of Persian pottery.   He bought white tiles, large dishes and pots from Staffordshire and painted them in *maiolica* style with strange but attractive designs, in harmonious colour schemes, of fantastic beasts and birds, fabulous ships under full sail (fig. 44) etc.   Tiles formed the bulk of his output but he made many vases and plaques and a beautiful set of dishes triple-lustred in copper, silver and gold.

Derby (c. 1749–1848)   Little is certain about Derby's origins as a small workshop where, in the 'Early Derby', 'dry-edge' or 'Planché' period (c. 1749–55), many unmarked figures were excellently modelled, traditionally by a young London Huguenot, André Planché, possibly financed by John Heath.   Paste and glaze were milk-white, the latter wiped away round the base to prevent figures sticking to kiln furniture—hence the term 'dry-edge figures'. They included *chinoiserie* figures (e.g. a set of 'Senses'), sophisticated shepherdesses and some boars and bulls, the best copied from Ancient Roman models. Many were left in the white. There are also mysterious white cream-jugs marked '1750 D(erby)', but little else survives.

The factory proper was established in Nottingham Road (1755) by William Duesbury, who had decorated for Chelsea, Bow and Derby in his London studio. His partners were Heath and possibly Planché (unmentioned after 1756). A shrewd businessman, Duesbury realized that it paid to advertise—as 'the second Dresden' (1757); he bought up Chelsea and possibly Bow and Longton Hall.

In the first three years he produced a transitional 'pale-coloured family' of delicate doll-like figures in lightweight chalky paste with blued glaze, decorated in pastel colours; the dry edge disappeared with Planché but another Planché hallmark, funnel-shaped base vents, continued. Figures were always Derby's mainstay, and the next generation was the 'patch family' (1758–70), typically with three or four patches marked on the base by clay balls on which figures rested in the kiln—a substitute for the dry edge precaution. These figures, thought until 1926 to be Chelsea, have numerous characteristics: knife-edge garment folds, sharp nose, flushed cheeks, and a dominant dirty turquoise. They imitated Chelsea Gold Anchor trends, and included classical groups and 'Ranelagh' figures (couples in fancy dress), some with BOCAGES. Useful wares are few but comprise attractive tea-sets, sauceboats, openware baskets and elaborate Meissen-style vases which became another Derby speciality, particularly of the Crown Derby period.

In the CHELSEA-DERBY years (1770–84) Derby employed fine artists, including Stéphan (figures of national heroes), Askew (cupids), Duvivier (landscapes), the young Billingsley and latterly Boreman (landscapes). Bone-ash was added to Bow-style paste. A highly successful innovation was the first, and best, English biscuit figures, more numerous than Crown Derby (fig. 15), some modelled by Spängler; 'smear' glazing imparted an ivory sheen, the glaze being smeared not on the figure but on the kiln walls, and volatilized. Figures were marked on the base with a script 'N' and model number. High-quality useful wares were made, often with Neo-Classical decoration, probably mainly for the cabinet, especially coffee cans.

On Duesbury's death his son, also William, inherited, initiating the *Crown Derby* period (1786–1811), named from the mark used. During the ten years before his death he put Derby in the forefront of English porcelain, helped by a finer translucent porcelain and clearer glaze, decorated by artists of the preceding period and by newcomers. His successor Kean upset the staff, the artists left and a general decline followed; bone china was introduced, permitting greater concentration on tablewares; much Imari decoration was used, and naturalistic life-size named flowers painted by 'Quaker' Pegg.

The final period is called *Bloor Derby* (1811–48), although the date that Richard Bloor bought the factory may have been 1814, and when he became insane in 1828 control passed to a useless manager. Bloor's main preoccupation was to pay off the mortgage by indiscriminate marketing of vast quantities of substandard stock, painted in heavy Imari patterns to hide defects, and to suit rising industrialists' tastes. But he also produced fine ware painted by new artists such as Thomas Steel (fruit) and Moses Webster (Billingsley-style flowers). There were also sentimental gaudy figures (Plate 7) and plaques.

After the main factory closed for good, some employees started an independent factory in King Street, the *Old Crown Derby China Works* (1848–1935), which under various managements copied old Derby patterns and used old moulds. The *Stevenson & Hancock* regime, continued by Sampson Hancock alone (*c.* 1865–98), was the most successful, producing many figures, old and new, and hand-painted JAPAN PATTERN tea-sets etc.

In 1876 an entirely new concern, the (*Royal*) *Crown Derby Porcelain Co.*, was established at Osmaston Road, and continues to this day (Plate 5). In 1935 it bought the King Street factory.

Dessert services Early sets would include plates, comports (i.e. pedestalled fruit-dishes), covered baskets with stands or pierced-work baskets, LEAF DISHES, covered cream, sugar and sauce tureens (with stand and ladle), two-handled covered ice-pails with liners, COMFIT-HOLDERS, and an elaborate centre-piece of several sweetmeat dishes grouped together on different levels.

Dinner services The standard 18th-century sets would include soup and meat plates, meat platters, salad bowls (also used as junket dishes), sauceboats and a covered tureen with stand and ladle, often a highly elaborate piece (see HEN TUREENS). There might also be hors-d'oeuvres sets of six dishes fitting round a centre dish, finger-bowls and stands, mustard pots and salts, and asparagus-servers. The *Monteith*, a bowl with deeply notched rim to take wine glasses resting inwards on ice, was usually of silver or glass but is sometimes found in porcelain.

The fashionable dinner-time advanced from about 3 p.m. in 1700 to 6 p.m. in 1770. Since breakfasts were minimal and there was no luncheon, dinners were gargantuan; a bishop in 1783 laid on two 'courses' of twenty dishes each followed by a dessert of twenty dishes. There might also be a supper at about 10 p.m.

Dr Syntax (1815) An accident-prone clergyman-schoolmaster whose tours on his nag Grizzle were depicted in a series of 80 plates by Thomas Rowlandson; William Combe, in a debtors' prison, wrote verse for each plate as it was finished, and the final result was three best-selling books, parodying the popular travel books of the day.

Incidents from the series appear on Staffordshire blue-and-white and Spode polychrome plates, in a series of 14 figures on circular bases made by Derby (1830), and as Staffordshire pottery figures (fig. 45).

Don Pottery (c. 1799–1893) A south Yorkshire pottery at Swinton, near Doncaster, founded by members of the Green family which had been connected with the Leeds Pottery, and sold in 1834 to the Barkers of Mexborough Pottery. They made good Leeds-type creamware, earthenware tea-sets with red or chocolate rims and painted decoration, green-glazed dessert services with moulded patterns, and blue-and-white wares with named and well-executed scenes of ancient Italy. Cow-creamers with coffee-coloured glaze and black markings are attributed to Don, perhaps on slender evidence. Marks may include the names Don, Green or Barker, or initials S.B. & S.

Doulton (1815–today) A Lambeth firm which manufactured brown saltglaze stoneware, at first for industrial use only. From the 1830s they also made decorative spirit flasks (see STONEWARE).

Doultons are celebrated for their revival (c. 1870) of individually designed and decorated collectors' pieces, a first step towards the STUDIO POTTERY movement; Henry Doulton, through friendship with the head of the Lambeth School of Art, was able to employ its students as decorators. These wares included stoneware vases, tankards, jugs, classical urns etc., decorated with coloured patterns of flowers and foliage in incised outline; rows of applied beads in white slip became an increasingly prominent feature.

Hannah Barlow, one of the most famous students, specialized in spirited animal sketches done in economically used incised outlines filled in with cobalt blue (fig. 46; see also SCRATCH BLUE); later she lost the use of her right arm and trained herself to use the left. Her sister Florence painted bird studies in coloured clays and also did incised work. *George Tinworth* made excellent terracotta plaques of biblical scenes, and also amusing animal groups, e.g. of mice watching

46 DOULTON Jar decorated by Hannah Barlow, 1883

74

a Punch and Judy show, and others illustrating Aesop's fables. All pieces bear the artist's signature, factory mark and (usually) date.

Doultons also made (1875–1914) what they called *faience*, i.e. creamware vases, dishes, tiles, plaques etc. painted underglaze; 'Silicon' (1880s), i.e. unglazed brown stoneware carved and decorated in various ways; 'Carrara', a dense white stoneware; '*impasto*' thickly painted on unfired clay; and, later, stoneware Toby-style 'character' jugs depicting celebrities.

In 1882 a factory at Burslem, Staffordshire, was taken over, where high-quality porcelain has been made until today; stoneware was discontinued in 1956.

Dressing-table sets An 18th-century set might comprise a porcelain tray (for brush and comb), a pair of porcelain candlesticks, powder and trinket bowls. The Victorians liked ring-stands in the shape of a hand, a branched tree or antlers, set in a pin-tray. From *c.* 1855 there were also pin-boxes made by the same firms and in the same style as FAIRINGS.

Drug-jars Made from the 17th century (in delft-ware), these jars stood in chemists' shops marked in abbreviated Latin with their contents. These and jars of succeeding centuries are found in many shapes and often bear elaborate decorations, e.g. Apollo as god of healing, cherubs and much scrollery. Originally there were no lids (they were covered with parchment if necessary). Those for oils and syrups had handles and spouts, but these were not needed for electuaries (powders in honey) and treacles (for poisonous bites). Abbreviated Latin names must have assisted sales of e.g. Oil of Puppydogs and Oil of Earthworms. See fig. 47.

Earthenware Porous non-vitrified baked clay; to make it of practical domestic use it has to be rendered impervious to liquids by glazing. Used from ancient times (e.g. for the terracotta figurines of Tanagra, *c.* 350 B.C.), its main forms in England, as the result of successive modifications, were SLIPWARE, DELFT-WARE (*c.* 1571), CREAMWARE (*c.* 1720), STONE CHINA (1805), MASON'S PATENT IRONSTONE (1813). It was also used in ASTBURY and allied wares.

Egg cups Attractive examples are found in First Period Worcester and Leeds creamware, and 19th-century services by Spode, Coalport etc. often included egg cups in matching designs, sometimes with stands.

Elers ware Unglazed smooth-surfaced red stone-ware, typically in the form of teapots with applied reliefs, originally made in imitation of Chinese wares (fig. 48). Traditionally attributed to David and

John Elers, who came to England from Holland about the time of William of Orange (1688) and worked in London and Staffordshire, they may also (or first) have been made by Dwight of Fulham, who patented an opaque red 'porcelain' in 1684 and later accused the Elers, among others, of infringing his patent. Elers-type wares were later made by other Staffordshire potters, e.g. Astbury.

Wedgwood attributed to the Elers the idea of using a lathe to achieve the exceptionally smooth finish on these pots, and other innovations such as SALTGLAZE (which is doubtful) and the addition of ground flints to the clay.

Fairings Small porcelain figure groups made in Germany for the English market *c.* 1850–1914 as six-penny presents for husbands to bring back from fair or market (fig. 49). Archly humorous inscriptions on the base tended to be on bedroom themes (hence the nickname 'Early-to-beds'). 'The last in bed to put out

49 FAIRINGS
'Kiss Me Quick'
(*Mary Payton
Antiques*)

the light' is the commonest; others are 'Shall We Sleep First or How', 'Mr Jones, remove your Hat' (said by a woman abed to a man in his nightshirt). Many were designed as match or watch holders. Rare specimens, e.g. those featuring velocipedes, fetch high prices, but others can be bought for a few pounds. Early examples usually have an incised or impressed number (starting at 2850); others have a trade mark and, after 1891, are marked 'Germany'. Guides to dating include style of lettering and gilding.

Fakes and forgeries Strictly speaking, while forgeries are 100% fraudulent, the much commoner fakes begin life as genuine pieces, bought in the white or sparsely decorated, then given new or additional decoration (any existing unwanted decoration being removed) designed to increase their value. For example, the rare yellow ground might be added to genuine early Worcester plates. A third category is the *reproduction*, a copy possibly made with honest intent but turned into a fake by removing a manufacturer's give-away mark or adding a false one. In practice these terms tend to get mixed up.

There are degrees of deceit: thus the 'C' on Caughley is suspiciously like the Worcester crescent; early Derby was left unmarked apparently in the hope that it would pass as Meissen or Chelsea; Worcester sometimes used Meissen or pseudo-Chinese marks, while Lowestoft used Worcester's; Coalport copied many factories.

Soft-paste porcelain is difficult to imitate, and most Continental copies of English 18th-century porcelain are in hard-paste and thus relatively easy to detect. *Samson of Paris* from the 1870s made accurate copies of Plymouth and Bristol hard-paste, Chelsea and

Derby, but they were marked 'S' (easily removed). Some were so good that they are now collected on their own merits.

Worcester was the chief victim, especially scale-blue; it was even reproduced in earthenware, by Booth (but marked 'B'). Red Anchor Chelsea was copied in bone china at Tournai, but most Chelsea forgeries are of Gold Anchor pieces, with the anchor too large and prominent. Nantgarw/Swansea forgeries are numerous, usually with overglaze painted marks. In recent years poor forgeries have been made of Chelsea and Derby birds and animals, also of porcelain and pottery cottages. Many were made by Creative Studios, Torquay, now defunct.

There have also been recent forgeries of Ralph Wood, Astbury and Whieldon figures. Most forgeries in pottery are difficult to spot, and all kinds have been imitated—delft, slipware, saltglaze, creamware, Wedgwood wares (lacking the mark) and lustre.

Famille rose etc. *Famille rose* is the name given to a 'family' of Chinese (Chi'en Lung) porcelain painted in a palette based on a new range of opaque pink enamels (derived from gold) invented in Europe but borrowed by the Chinese for use on export porcelain (*c.* 1725–1795). It was decorated in a delicate style of minia-ture-like refinement, with the addition of other semi-opaque enamels, especially blue and yellow. The basic rose-pink could be changed to rose-purple or violet by altering the kiln temperature. This style was copied by Meissen, Bow, Chelsea, Worcester etc.

Famille verte was an earlier, K'ang Hsi (1662–1722), 'family' decorated in transparent enamels, with green and iron-red predominating, supplemented by yellow, violet-blue and aubergine. Introduced *c.* 1700, it was imitated on Continental and English porcelain.

Famille noire was *famille verte* painted on a lustrous green-black ground colour.

Ferrybridge (1792)   A pottery near Pontefract, Yorkshire, established by William Tomlinson which made various wares in close imitation of Wedgwood (creamware, cameos, green-glaze ware etc.), added to by stamping them 'Wedgwood & Co.' after taking on Josiah's cousin Ralph Wedgwood as partner (1796). The marks 'Tomlinson & Co.' and (after 1804) 'Ferrybridge' were also used.   The pottery continued under various names until the present century.

Figures   The high fashion for porcelain figures was extraordinarily short-lived.   In about 1750, less than twenty years after the great Kändler began his career at Meissen, there was a sudden outburst of figure production at Chelsea, Bow, Derby and Longton Hall; but by 1777 only Derby survived, to continue making enamelled figures for provincials who lagged behind the (London) times, and also introducing BISCUIT figures.   Worcester in its earlier days made very few. In 1768 Plymouth and Bristol began to make some not very satisfactory hard-paste examples.

The fashion had been to group these figures on dining or dessert table, but *c.* 1760 a new type was introduced, intended to be viewed from the front only and used as cabinet exhibits or chimney-piece ornaments. Thus the BOCAGE background came into favour; the ultimate development of this trend was to be the Victorian flat-back.   In the 19th century figures in PARIAN or stoneware came to be preferred; in porcelain the chief names are Derby (Plate 7), Rockingham, Minton and Royal Worcester.

50 FIGURES Set of Seasons, Chelsea-Derby

The potters had anticipated the porcelain makers—
SALTGLAZE figures were made from c. 1730; see also
ASTBURY WARE; WOOD FAMILY; WALTON SCHOOL;
STAFFORDSHIRE FIGURES, PRE-VICTORIAN and VIC-
TORIAN; LEEDS etc.

The range of subjects was very wide. There were
Chinese groups and figures, Classical gods and heroes;
the inevitable 'Dresden' shepherdesses, Turks, hunts-
men, gardeners, cooks, fishermen, usually paired off
with 'mates'; religious subjects, nuns; Matrimony,
Liberty, Charity etc. There were sets of Seasons
(fig. 50), represented by men, women, children or
putti—Spring holding flowers, Summer a wheatsheaf,
Autumn fruit, Winter skating or a figure huddling
from the cold. Sets of Continents show Asia as a
lady with a dog-sized camel, America as an 'Indian'
huntress with prairie dog, Africa as a negress with lion
and crocodile, Europe with a horse and crowned. In
the Elements, figures hold a bird (Air), burning-glass
(Fire) etc. The Five Senses have Sight with an eagle,
Scent with a dog etc. See also ANIMALS AND BIRDS;
COMMEDIA DELL' ARTE; MONKEY BAND.

The Staffordshire potter copied many of these

81

themes, but introduced elements normally missing in porcelain: a nearer approach to realism—looks and clothes were less courtly and a decrepit 'Old Age' was a favourite—and humour (see STAFFORDSHIRE GROUPS; SHERRATT, OBADIAH).

The making of a figure could be very complicated. The artist's wax model was cut into sections from which separate plaster moulds were taken. Hollow moulds (e.g. for the body) had slip (liquid porcelain) poured into them ('slip-casting'), which left a thin coat of porcelain on the plaster. Accessories (e.g. legs) were cast solid. All these casts, while still moist ('cheese-hard'), had to be quickly assembled by the 'repairer' and bonded together with slip.

The first firing followed, during which the porcelain would shrink by an eighth; the main difficulty was that all the parts had to shrink by the same amount, otherwise the figure would crack. This was why all these operations required great skill, encouraged in the bad old days before 1871 by the refusal to pay for work done on pieces that did not survive the kiln. After firing, glaze was painted on and fired; then enamels and gilding were painted on, each fired separately according to its resistance to heat. Bow figures in 1760 were sold undecorated to an enameller at from 10d. each ('Nuns and Fryers' being cheapest).

Flight & Barr Worcester (1793–1840) High standards were maintained in the period that succeeded WORCESTER (FIRST PERIOD) after Martin Barr joined the firm; owing to changes in partnership, this is subdivided into Flight & Barr (1793–1807), Barr, Flight & Barr (1807–13) and Flight, Barr & Barr (1813–40) periods. The factory was then absorbed by CHAMBERLAIN'S WORCESTER.

The Davis/Flight soapstone body continued in use even after the introduction, c. 1800, of bone china, which attained perfection of whiteness and translucency c. 1820. In conformity with fashion, Neo-Classical styles of decoration (urns, festoons, scrolls) were adopted. From c. 1807 shell motifs, printed or painted by Baxter and others, were popular; also, as at Derby, elaborate cabinet pieces, e.g. two-handled vases, open or covered, on square plinths, sometimes richly decorated with JAPAN PATTERNS or naturalistically painted flowers, many pieces being heavily gilded. Large dinner and dessert services (Plate 4), vases, *jardinières*, inkstandishes etc. were often decorated with named local landscapes or Angelica Kaufmann subjects, some by Baxter, and on new salmon-pink, claret or apple-green grounds.

Flower-holders and bulb-pots Bowls with perforated covers were used both for growing bulbs and for arranging flowers. They were made in a great variety of shapes and wares. 'Quintals' (fig. 51) were five-socketed fan-shaped holders on square bases used in the 18th century for tulips; they were made by Leeds (creamware) and Staffordshire potters. Similar holders were flat-backed to hang on walls. See CORNUCOPIA. One form was the *vase-in-hand*, a small vase held in a lady's hand, her cuff forming the base.

Food-warmers A bedside device (probably of Continental origin) to provide light and to keep drinks warm through the night; made in England from the 1770s to 1840s in delftware, creamware, porcelain etc., and often elaborately decorated. A lamp was placed in a large opening at the side of the base component, on which rested the covered pot containing the liquid (fig. 52). Sometimes a vessel of hot water was interposed between pot and lamp; in later types ('tea-warmers') the top element might be a teapot. The original purpose was to keep warm POSSET POTS AND CAUDLE CUPS; there were also toddy-warmers, presumably on the other side of the bed. Another variety of food-warmer was the double-thickness plate with a hole in the rim, into which hot water or hot sand could be poured.

Footbath A pottery bowl about 9 in. (230 mm) deep and perhaps 18×14 in. (450×350 mm) wide, sometimes with handles. Made by most potters in the 19th century, when our forebears were addicted to mustard baths for tired feet, many footbaths were surprisingly well decorated; now that feet are no longer used, they make attractive containers for plants and flowers. Early specimens have straight sides; after *c.* 1830 convex.

Frog-mugs Quaint reminders of 18th-century tavern humour. Theoretically the guileless toper would be startled as he lowered his ale to see a frog (often gaudily spotted) peering out of the dregs or crawling up the drinking side; in early mugs the frog might be hollowed to produce gurgling sounds as the beer spouted from its open mouth. These mugs were made from *c.* 1750 to the 1880s, particularly in Sunderland and Staffordshire (fig. 53), and have since been reproduced. Some had more than one frog, a few had toads, snakes or newts.

Fruit and vegetables These have often been re-produced in porcelain and pottery, sometimes as dishes (e.g. a Chelsea apple sliced so that the top half can be lifted by its stalk) or just for fun (e.g. cucum-

51 (*above*) FLOWER-HOLDERS
Pink lustre quintal tulip vase,
c. 1810 (*Delomosne & Son*)

52 (*above*) FOOD-
WARMERS A Bristol
delftware example *c.* 1760
(*Sotheby & Co.*)

53 (*above*) FROG-MUGS Interior
of fig. 115 (*Mary Payton Antiques*)

54 (*below*) FRUIT AND
VEGETABLES Miniature
cucumber, Whieldon
green-glaze, *c.* 1755 (*City
Museum, Stoke-on-Trent*)

bers; fig. 54). Other lidded forms are cos lettuce, globe artichoke, cauliflower, lemon, orange, bundle of asparagus and melon.

Fulham Pottery This London pottery, founded by John Dwight (1671; see SALTGLAZE), remained in his family till 1861, and is still producing stonewares. In 1877 Dwight's original formula was still being used in making stoneware figures; terracotta figures were also made, some perhaps modelled by Wallace Martin (see MARTINWARE) when he was there in 1872.

Gaudy Welsh (1830–60) American name for cheap pottery ware made, probably in Swansea, mainly for the U.S. market. It was gaily decorated with a characteristic floral design in orange, blue and gold.

Girl-in-a-swing factory (c. 1751–54) Probably founded, in Chelsea, by a breakaway group of work-men who left the main Chelsea factory on change of management; so called from a figure of this subject identified as coming from it (now in the Victoria and Albert Museum, London). Little is known of the factory, but its products are now confidently identified, mainly consisting of attractive small figures and the highly valued, delightful miniature 'Chelsea toys' (e.g. scent-bottles (fig. 55), *bonbonnières*, seals etc. in the form of animals, birds, *putti* etc.) of the type that Chelsea itself later manufactured in its gold anchor period. The very thin glaze permitted great clarity of detailed outline, resulting in a distinctive style, especially in modelling faces and drapery.

Goss (1858–1929) W. H. Goss made his reputation as an artist at Copelands before setting up his own

pottery at Stoke. Here, in 'ivory porcelain' (a kind of PARIAN), he made portrait busts, statues, ear-rings and brooches shaped as flowers, and 'jewelled' pieces in which gems were embedded. About 1893 he started a very successful line of translucent well-decorated cottages (Anne Hathaway's, Burns's etc.), meticulously accurate in detail; pre-1914 examples, bearing a 6-digit registration number, are prized by collectors.

To most, 'Goss' means the crested or heraldic china

started c. 1884, eggshell-thin miniature pieces transfer-printed with the crest of some popular seaside resort—the poor man's cabinet piece. The range of shapes was great; those who like oddities may look for e.g. models of a Cornish pasty marked Lostwithiel, or of Queen Victoria's first little shoe, bought by father at Sidmouth, and bearing the Sidmouth crest.

The firm passed into various hands after 1929; quality deteriorated but the Goss mark was retained.

Grainger's Worcester (1800–89) Founded by Thomas Grainger who had decorated for his father-in-law Robert Chamberlain (see CHAMBERLAIN'S WORCESTER). Like him, Grainger at first decorated porcelain bought from other factories, but in 1812, as Grainger, Lee & Co., he began to make a fine translucent porcelain and produce wares in the Chamberlain and, later, Royal Worcester styles; early specimens are not easily identifiable as they were usually unmarked. Other products were 'Semi-Porcelain', an opaque earthenware (fig. 56); cabinet pieces in Parian ware or PÂTE-SUR-PÂTE; and LITHOPHANES. The factory was bought out by the Royal Worcester Porcelain Co.

Green-glazed wares Wedgwood, while working with Whieldon, perfected the first of several semi-translucent green lead glazes c. 1760, used typically as an all-over glaze on dessert plates moulded with leaf designs etc. These proved very popular, and similar wares were made from c. 1837 by Rockingham, Don Pottery and Copeland. Wedgwood still makes them.

Hen tureens Tureens in the form of a hen and chickens, partridge (fig. 57), other birds, rabbits or

57 HEN TUREENS
Derby partridge
tureen

fish etc. were copied from Meissen models by Chelsea, Bow and Derby *c.* 1750–70 for use as sweetmeat dishes. They reappeared in the 1820s as vividly coloured 'hens-on-nests'; small models might originally have contained a Valentine gift (Plate 8). Most of those found today are Staffordshire pottery hens of the 1840s to 1860s; they were fair prizes filled with sweets. Others in bone china or Parian ware kept boiled eggs warm at the breakfast table.

Inkstandish 'Stand-dish' itself once meant 'inkstand', but by the 18th century the accepted name became inkstandish. It comprised accessories which reflect the complexities of letter-writing in those days; porcelain inkstandishes imitated earlier silver models.

The tray would contain some of the following. An inkpot surrounded by holes for spare quills; the holes might contain lead-shot for cleansing the clotted quill-tip, or there might be a separate quill-cleaner. A 'sand' box, a kind of pepper-pot originally for powdered gum sandarac (hence the name); this had to be poured on to the oily surface of parchment before it could be written on. It became a real sand-box in the 1790s when glossy paper came in; black sand was peppered over the slow-drying ink. A

89

pounce-dredger with fine powder for rubbing on to mistakes scratched out with a penknife, thus restoring the surface; 'pounce' meant 'powdered pumice' originally. A wafer-box for little red seals (made of flour) put on unimportant letters; Victorians put stamps in this.   A taper-holder for use in wax-sealing *billets-doux* etc.   A covered tray for penknife, pencil, seals, wax etc.   And finally, 'for the man who has to have everything', a little bell to summon a servitor to deliver the missive by hand. The whole, elaborately decorated in blue (against ink-stains) and gilt, even flower-encrusted, was so attractive that one feels it was never actually used. (Fig. 58.)

Jackfield ware (1740–80)   A generic term misused for almost anything black and glossy, most frequently seen in the form of COW-CREAMERS of uncertain youth.   Strictly, the name refers to red earthenware darkened with manganese and cobalt, thickly coated with very shiny glaze and, typically, decorated solely by linseed oil-based gilding mostly or wholly rubbed off in use.   Traditionally attributed to the Jackfield factory in Shropshire (bought up by Coalport, 1780), it was also made by several Staffordshire potteries, including Whieldon's.   Wares included coffee and teapots, jugs (fig. 59) etc.

Japan patterns   A term best reserved for designs on English porcelain and pottery derived, usually very distantly, from one of two quite different Japanese styles: Kakiemon and Imari.   It is however sometimes used of other oriental, including Chinese, patterns, all of which in the 18th century tended to be lumped together as 'Japanese' or even 'Indian'.

Kakiemon was the founder of a family of potters who worked in the Arita district of Japan *c.* 1650–1720.

58 (*above*) INKSTANDISH A Coalport flower-encrusted inkstand *c.* 1815–20 (*Sotheby & Co.*)

59 (*above*) JACKFIELD WARE Coffee pot, *c.* 1760–80 (*Godden of Worthing*)

60 (*right*) JASPER WARE Vase modelled by Flaxman depicting 'The Apotheosis of Homer', *c.* 1786 (*Wedgwood Museum*)

His style, derived from the Chinese, was characterized by unsymmetrical compositions of well-spaced flowering branches (especially *Prunus*) with additions such as rocks, banded hedges (the Worcester 'wheatsheaf'), quails (which were called partridges in England) etc. These were painted in a pleasing palette of brick-red, green and lilac, often supplemented by yellow, turquoise, gilding or underglaze blue. Sparingly applied, this decoration emphasized the perfection of white porcelain. It was copied by Meissen, Bow, Chelsea, Worcester etc.

Imari is a later and much less refined style, named from the Arita district's port, indicating that it was used on exports only. The palette was dark underglaze blue and indian red enamel, combined with much gilding in confused patterns covering every inch of space available, featuring chrysanthemums, paeonies and also dragons, the Ho-ho bird and other CHINOISERIES. It was inspired by oriental brocaded silks and lacquer, which caught European fancy. Imari ware was already being shipped by the Dutch in large quantities by 1700; it was copied by Meissen, Bow and Worcester (where the brocaded designs were called 'mosaics').

As an all-over pattern it was useful in covering up defects on bone china and became a Derby speciality under Bloor and Royal Crown Derby (Plate 5 and fig. 118), the latter avidly collected by gypsies for its golden glitter; but the most garish examples came from Chamberlain's Worcester. Spode, Davenport and Mason's Ironstone also featured this style.

Jardinières Ornamental flower-pots; some were urn or vase shaped and they were a favourite subject for art potteries.

61 (*right*) JUGS
Sussex pottery
pig with
detachable head
(*Brighton Art
Gallery and
Museums*)

62 (*left*) JUGS Worcester
blue and gold cabbage-
leaf mask jug, Flight/
Davis period, *c.* 1783–88
(*Dyson Perrins Museum,
Worcester*)

63 (*below, left*) LEAF
DISHES Longton Hall
twig-handled lettuce-leaf
dish (*Sotheby & Co.*)
64 (*below, right*) LEAF
DISHES Blue-and-white
First Period Worcester
c. 1755

Jasper ware (1776)   A dense unglazed stoneware, translucent when thin; the white body was either colour-stained throughout or surface-coloured by dipping.   It was invented by Josiah WEDGWOOD I as a challenge to Champion's monopoly of hard-paste porcelain ingredients (see CHAMPION'S BRISTOL). Decoration was in white relief, classical themes predominating; wares included vases (fig. 60), tea-sets, portrait medallions, plaques and a variety of small objects.   Wedgwood employed some famous artists (e.g. Flaxman, 1776–87) to design the reliefs.   The commonest colour is blue, pale at first and today, but darker in the 1800s; there is also jasper in green, black or a combination of colours.   In the earlier examples the moulded clay reliefs are trimmed up by hand cutting to obtain sharper relief.   An outstanding example was a series of exact copies of the Portland Vase in blue-black (1790), reissued later in blue. Jasper ware was imitated by many other potters.

Jugs   Of the infinite variety of jugs, some of the best-known are the sharp-pointed sparrow-beak cream jugs (Worcester etc.), masked-lip jugs in moulded cabbage-leaf form (Worcester, Caughley etc.; fig. 62), the helmet-shaped cream-jug (New Hall etc.), the octagonal jug in MASON'S PATENT IRONSTONE, and many examples in BROWNWARE.   Narrow-necked *harvest jugs*, taken out to the men at work at haymaking and harvest seasons, were made in stoneware or earthenware, sometimes covered with slipware and inscribed with appropriate doggerel.   Each region had its own style (fig. 61).   See also PUZZLE JUG; APOSTLE JUG; BELLARMINES; NOTTINGHAM WARE; COW-CREAMERS.

Kerr & Binns   See CHAMBERLAIN'S WORCESTER.

Knife-rests Usually metal but sometimes found in well-decorated pottery; the original purpose was to keep the used knife and fork off the table while courses were changed. As in parts of France today, the same implements were retained through the meal.

Leaf dishes Small moulded porcelain trays in the form of a leaf, made by most factories from the 18th century onwards to hold sauces, ginger, pickles etc. Bow favoured vine leaves, Worcester overlapping cabbage leaves or a vine leaf with the stalk forming a handle, Longton Hall twig handles and Caughley ivy leaves (figs. 63 and 64). Similar are the scallop shells made by Liverpool, Worcester etc.

Leeds Pottery (c. 1760–1878) Chiefly noted for fine CREAMWARE, especially the pierce work of the 1780–1820 period. Unfortunately it was copied, together with the Leeds mark, by at least three firms, including Slee of Leeds (1888–1916) whose products have a pinkish tinge and are altogether too light; other fakes were too thick, and badly crazed, and those with transfer-printed subjects of American interest were too brilliant. It is said that the genuine mark, an impressed 'Leeds Pottery', is in capitals which taper off in size, which the faked marks do not.

Leeds made a wide range of creamware figures (some, in the 1790s, in PEARLWARE), including birds, animals, Derby-style gods, musicians, the Four Elements, Isaac Newton, making free use of Staffordshire models. The large piebald horses of the early 1800s are particularly well known (fig. 65); they originally advertised shops selling harness or veterinary drugs. This factory also made basalt, lustre, red, Jackfield and saltglaze wares. It went bankrupt in 1820 but was kept in production by others.

Linthorpe Pottery (1879–89) A Yorkshire art pottery at Middlesbrough, where the local coarse red clay was used for pottery (often of almost surrealistic shapes) decorated with beautiful iridescent many-coloured flowing glazes and SGRAFFITO. The tone was set by Henry Tooth, who was there for only three years. Artists drew inspiration from the ancient art of Egypt, the Far East or Central America, or from the Middle Ages, and each item was individually fashioned (fig. 66).

Lithophanes (1827–c. 1910) Thin white porcelain panels of varying thickness which, when (but only when) held to the light, reveal a detailed black-and-white mezzotint-like picture that might be of a land-scape, battle or scene from fiction but was more frequently a religious subject. The effect was achieved by a laborious process of modelling a wax mould (from which successive plaster and metal moulds were taken) to obtain minutely different thicknesses in the porcelain—the highlights very thin, the shadows comparatively thick.

Lithophanes were incorporated in lamp shades, night-light holders, fire-screens or the base of a mug, or were made to be hung in windows. Most are German (marked KPM, PPM etc.), but at the height of their popularity in the 1850s some were made by Minton, Grainger (Worcester), Copeland, Belleek and other firms in Britain and elsewhere (fig. 67). (Coined Greek word, 'see-through stone'.)

Liverpool There were several porcelain factories in Liverpool, specializing mainly in hard-wearing blue-and-white wares, especially mugs and jugs, for

PLATE 1 (*above*) Tithe Pig group, WALTON SCHOOL
(see STAFFORDSHIRE GROUPS)

(*below*) Victoria and Albert, *c.* 1843 (see
STAFFORDSHIRE FIGURES, VICTORIAN)

(*left*) Early PRATT-WARE jug

PLATE 2

(*below*) Swansea dish, marked. Mandarin pattern (see NANTGARW/SWANSEA; CHINOISERIE)

(*above*) DAVENPORT
vases, marked, *c.* 1856

PLATE 3

(*centre left*) Flower-
encrusted vase, de-
corated by and marked
'Doe & Rogers, Wor-
cester', 1820–40 (see
COALBROOKDALE)

(*right*) COALPORT
christening mug

PLATE 4   FLIGHT, BARR & BARR (Worcester) tureen,
marked, c. 1813–40

PLATE 5   (*above*) SPODE coffee cup and saucer

(*below*) Royal Crown DERBY coffee cup and
saucer, Imari JAPAN PATTERN

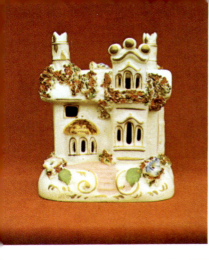

(*left*) Pastille bur-
ner, Staffordshire
(see COTTAGES)

PLATE 6

(*below*) POT-LID,
'Il Penseroso'

PLATE 7   Bloor DERBY group 'The Shoeblack', c. 1835

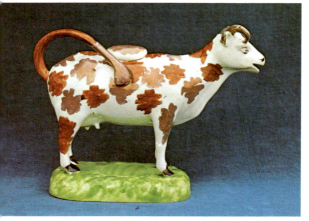

PLATE 8   (*above*) Hen-on-nest, Staffs. miniature (see
HEN TUREENS)

(*below*) Swansea COW-CREAMER; LUSTRE-
WARE

66 (*right*) LINTHORPE POTTERY
Brown glaze vase by
Christopher Dresser (*Teesside
Museum*)

65 (*above*) LEEDS POTTERY
Pearlware horse (*Leeds City
Art Galleries*)

67 (*below*) LITHOPHANE
View of the Rhine (*Mary
Payton Antiques*)

markets in northern England and America. Few were marked, and attribution to specific factories is particularly difficult as many features, though typical of Liverpool, are common to several of them. These include a greyish look; barrel-shaped mugs with a concave band near the base, jug lips higher than the rim; masked-lip jugs in which the face is younger than the Caughley type; red transfer-printing; handles with prominent thumb-rests; odd, sometimes humorous, Chinese scenes. The relatively few enamel-painted pieces tend to garishness; there are hardly any figures.

Soapstone porcelain was used by Richard Chaffers (1754–65) and his successor Philip Christian (1765–1776), also by William Reid (c. 1755–61) and William Ball (c. 1755–69); bone-ash porcelain by Seth Pennington (c. 1769–1805) and Samuel Gilbody (c. 1754–61); bone china at the Herculaneum factory (1793–1840); and near-hard paste porcelain by Thomas Wolfe (c. 1790–1800).

Chaffers's products included the earliest transfer-prints, in black, brown or red. Christian added to the Chaffers range elaborate moulded shapes and good enamel-painted wares. Pennington (fig. 68) copied some of Christian's designs but in the 1790s turned to mass production of cruder stuff. Gilbody's porcelain resembled Longton Hall; attractive bird designs and *chinoiseries* are attributed to this factory. Reid's products resembled Lund's Bristol and featured blue-and-white printed with European scenes, floral designs in *famille rose*, moulded wares and fine teapots. William Ball's speciality was 'polychrome prints', i.e. printed outlines in pink, brown or black, in which were painted Meissen flowers or insects and European or Chinese figure scenes, later copied by Champion's

68 LIVERPOOL Miniature teapot, coffee cup and saucer. Pennington. *c.* 1785 (*From a private collection*)

Bristol. Other features were Imari designs, Bow-like blue-and-white sauceboats and many small items such as inkstands, candlesticks etc. Wolfe's porcelain, resembling New Hall, was clumsily potted and usually decorated with transfer-prints in various colours; handles are ungainly. Herculaneum produced much domestic ware transfer-printed with named views etc.; also urn-shaped vases, busts (in porcelain and stoneware) and some crude figures decorated blue and yellow.

Sadler & Green (1756–99) decorated wares with black or red transfer prints for other factories, including Liverpool and Longton Hall porcelain and Wedgwood and other Staffordshire pottery.

As to **pottery**, delftwares, notably punchbowls, were made from 1710; saltglaze, cream-coloured earthenware and stoneware were also made. Most of the factories mentioned above made pottery before and after turning to porcelain.

London decorators Independent enamellers and gilders of porcelain who decorated wares which they bought from, or which were sent to them by, the major 18th-century factories, either 'in the white' (i.e. glazed but not decorated) or partially decorated, e.g. in underglaze blue. They tended to decorate in a more sophisticated Continental style than the factories' own artists. Some of them seem eventually to have been lured into at least short-term employment by individual firms. Their activities have made life much more difficult for connoisseurs, intensifying their disagreements over attributions.

The most famous were the artists of the *Giles studio* (c. 1760–78), established by James Giles in Kentish Town and later Soho. Giles's own work has not been identified, and his highly gifted artists are only known by such unsatisfying names as the 'spotted-fruit painter' (on Derby), the 'sliced-fruit painter' (on Worcester), the painter of 'dishevelled birds' (mainly Worcester) or of 'open-petalled tulips'. This studio was chiefly associated with Worcester, but also decorated for most other factories. Their decorations included armorial, landscape, scenes taken from Watteau or Teniers, and ground colours, executed according to the instructions of private buyers or the manufacturers. Giles went bankrupt and William Duesbury (see DERBY) took over the studio.

Possibly a member of this group was *Jeffryes Hamett O'Neale*, who specialized in Aesop's fables and landscapes; his work appears on Chelsea (c. 1750), Worcester and Wedgwood, sometimes signed. Another possible member was *Fidelle Duvivier*, who came from France c. 1763; his style resembled O'Neale's and he seems to have worked on (or at) Chelsea, Derby, Worcester and Caughley.

John Donaldson was a miniaturist who came to London in 1760; his signed work appears on Chelsea and he also worked for Worcester and Derby.

Later in the century the Worcester-born *Baxters* had a workshop at Clerkenwell and decorated Coalport, Caughley and Worcester. The son, Thomas, also worked at Worcester and Swansea (1814–21).

Long Elizas English nickname for the tall and elegant ladies who featured prominently on 18th-century Chinese (K'ang-Hsi) blue-and-white porcelain exported to the West; they were copied on delftware by the Dutch (who called them *Lange Lijzen*, 'tall stupids'; corrupted to 'Long Elizas'), on early Worcester and much other blue-and-white and polychrome (fig. 69).

Longton Hall (*c.* 1749–60) The first Staffordshire porcelain factory, near Stoke; William Littler, who had worked in saltglaze, was the moving spirit of its brief existence, maintaining a large output despite financial crises. The Longton Hall body was usually heavy, thickly and unevenly potted, with greenish translucency showing many 'moons'. The glaze at first was thin, with a cold white glitter and many

69 LONG ELIZAS Worcester (First Period) blue-and-white vases *c.* 1760–65 (*Sotheby & Co.*)

black specks.

Many pieces were decorated, even swamped, in a streaky underglaze dark blue ('Littler's blue'), e.g. a white plate might have a solid blue moulded border; a yellowish green was another characteristic colour. Leaf-shaped dishes (fig. 63), and sauceboats moulded with high-relief overlapping leaves (fig. 70), were common. Decoration (and general quality) improved in the middle years with the arrival of William Duesbury (later of Derby) as enameller, the 'Trembly Rose' painter and another who specialized in castles and classical ruins. Kakiemon patterns, the *famille rose* palette, a powder-blue ground and a better underglaze blue were among the new features.

Figures were important in the earliest and latest years only. The early ones form a group ('snowmen') of white figures mainly of animals (e.g. bulls, horses), Chinese and Greek deities or Meissen models; the thick exceptionally glassy glaze obscured the rather primitive modelling, and formed masses of bubbles; firecracks were prevalent. The later examples were quite different, better modelled, often large and massive figures, e.g. of the Continents, Seasons, musicians etc., with rather harsh colouring. Cookworthy appears to have obtained their moulds, for they were copied at Plymouth and Bristol.

Littler went to Scotland and set up shop at West Pans near Musselburgh, where he decorated old Longton Hall stock, some of which now fetch high prices. He died in great poverty.

Loving-cup A two-handled cup usually urn-shaped like a sporting trophy; it developed from the grace-cup passed round after grace at the end of a banquet. A silver version is still used at City of London functions etc., a footman carefully wiping the rim after each guest has sipped.

Loving-cups were made from the 1740s in white saltglaze (fig. 72), slipware, creamware, brownware etc., some transfer-printed in blue-and-white, or inscribed with the owner's name and a date, or the arms of a friendly society etc. Their more homely use, confined to northern and midland counties, was to enable two cronies, the cup between them, to take turn and turn about ('hob-nobbing', from *hob and nob*, 'give and take') sipping hot toddy (rum, sugar, lemon, nutmeg and water, much in favour 1780–1850). These cups are still made, e.g. at Rye in Sussex.

71 LOWESTOFT Teapot painted in underglaze blue

Lowestoft (1757–c. 1799)   A small factory catering mainly for an undemanding local middle class, and specializing in tea services (fig. 71) and commemorative pieces.   The paste, of local clay, resembled Bow in its high bone-ash content, had a creamy appearance and was more open-grained than most of its contemporaries; the glaze was laid on thickly enough to pool, and much of it had a bluish tint.

Products of the first four years are rarely seen, even in museums.   Until c. 1774 all wares were decorated in underglaze blue with 'Chinese' themes; some, e.g. sauceboats and tea-caddies (fig. 113), were additionally moulded in relief.   Most typical are the dated and named mugs, inkwells etc., commissioned to commemorate some event or person, and pieces marked 'A Trifle from Lowestoft' (or other local town).   Another curiosity was small circular plaques, apparently given to employees on the birth of a child.

Later, transfer-printed local views, ships, hunting scenes etc., came in, together with a bid for the London market in the form of wares well painted in enamels with floral designs in which a tulip or a rose (from the town's arms) was prominent.   There were a very few figures, and some animals and birds.

The 'Trifles' and other pieces have been much reproduced; on the other hand Lowestoft in its later years copied both the wares and the marks of other factories.   Further confusion was created by an employee, Robert Allen, who set up his own Lowestoft shop and decorated wares bought in the white from Leeds, Castleford and Staffordshire; he decorated them in the Lowestoft style and even added 'A Trifle from Lowestoft' to some.   The delightfully unassuming Lowestoft firm, when competition grew burden-

72 (*left*)
LOVING-CUP
Staffordshire
saltglaze, scratch
blue, 1748 (*City
Museum, Stoke-
on-Trent*)

73 (*above*) 'MAJOLICA'
Wedgwood green-glazed
plate, *c*. 1860 (*Victoria
and Albert Museum*)

74 (*right*) LUSTREWARE
Staffordshire silver-resist
jug, *c*. 1825 (*City
Museum, Stoke-on-Trent*)

some, diversified into curing herrings. See CHINESE
'LOWESTOFT'.

Lund's Bristol (c. 1748–52) The predecessor of
Worcester in the making of soapstone soft-paste porcelain, at a factory founded by Benjamin Lund on the
site of Lowdin's glassworks (and hence formerly called
Lowdin's Bristol). Not much has survived that can
be definitely assigned to Bristol rather than the earliest
Worcester years; very few pieces are marked. The
porcelain is usually greyish, but some is creamy white
and very translucent.

Sauceboats are the most numerous, some moulded
and decorated in underglaze blue; they always have a
thumb-rest on the handle. There were also cream
jugs, mugs, leaf-dishes, bowls, hexagonal globular
bottles and small vases. Chinese designs by the 'fine-
brush painter' are attractive, and others with polychrome oriental designs outlined in black; there are no
transfer-printed wares, no gilding, and only one set of
figures (a Chinese Immortal), in white, is known.

The firm and equipment were bought by Worcester,
and Lund moved there with his employees.

Lustreware An exclusively English form of ceramic
decoration with pigments containing minute quantities
of gold (for 'copper' and pink lustre) or platinum (for
'silver' lustre), together with various other ingredients.
Lustre is applied to bone china, creamware and other
kinds of pottery. There are several claimants to the
invention, which was first put to commercial use
c. 1800, the main centres of production being Staffordshire, Sunderland, Swansea, Newcastle, Leeds and
Liverpool (Herculaneum factory). All kinds of
things were lustred, including goblets, cottages, Toby

jugs, animals, frog mugs and puzzle jugs.

The original intention, to imitate the colour and shapes of gold and silver ware by all-over lustre inside and out, was abandoned, especially after electroplating was invented (1840), and lustreware developed as a thing of beauty in its own right. The most highly prized is silver resist, in which designs or reserve panels were formed, before the lustre was applied, by smearing them over with wax or grease that would protect them from (or 'resist') the lustre (fig. 74). These reserves might be left white or given a coloured ground (canary or blue are most sought), and further embellished by painting or transfer printing flowers, foliage, birds, landscapes, sporting scenes etc. In a reverse process, lustre was stencilled on.

The lustre was laid on as a very thin film; thus the colour of the body of the ware was important. Most copper lustre is painted on brown-glazed earthenware, as on the familiar copper lustre jug. A thin gold solution on white produced pink lustre, which could be deepened to purple by additional coats. 'Splashed' (mottled) pink or purple lustre was produced by dropping oil on to a wet 'copper' lustre; this type is particularly associated with SUNDERLAND. Wedgwood (c. 1805) produced a 'Moonlight lustre' of pink or purple, marbled with grey, brown or yellow.

Swansea (Cambrian and Glamorgan Potteries) is particularly associated with cow-creamers on green bases, the cows spotted with pink lustre and enamel colours (Plate 8). In Staffordshire, Spode, Wood & Caldwell, Davenport, Wedgwood and many others made lustreware, but attribution is difficult as much is unmarked.

Among the delights of lustreware are the doggerel

and mottoes dealing with anything from the sailor's farewell to trade, political elections, pious admonitions and plain bawdy. 'Sweet, Oh! Sweet is that Sensation, When two hearts in union meet' may serve to indicate the form. Some pieces celebrated current events and personalities. The best quality must be sought with patience; much of that seen is undistinguished or far from antique, and modern reproductions abound.

Madeley (c. 1825–40) A small factory near Coalport founded by Thomas Randall, who had worked at Caughley, Derby and Pinxton before setting up a decorating establishment in London specializing in decorating white or partly decorated Sèvres. He catered successfully for a revived vogue for 18th-century soft-paste Sèvres, making excellent imitations of it but, being a Quaker, refusing to fake the Sèvres mark. Among his decorators were his nephew John Randall, whose bird-paintings won him fame at Rockingham and Coalport, and William Cook (flowers), who also went on to Coalport. It is possible that Randall used the NANTGARW-SWANSEA formula obtained from his neighbour BILLINGSLEY just before the latter died. Only one marked piece has been found.

'Majolica' (1850) Minton's name for a family of earthenware moulded in bold relief and coated in coloured glazes (usually green; fig. 73). The modelling and painting, in academic style, was done by leading artists; dishes with vegetable shapes, *jardinières* and figures were among the more notable items made. Very little had any resemblance to Italian Renaissance *maiolica*, on which (see DELFTWARE) the decoration

75 MANSION HOUSE DWARF Staffordshire pottery version

was painted on to an opaque tin glaze. Wedgwood and most other potters borrowed the name for these cheaply and mass-produced wares. See DELLA ROBBIA WARE; 'PALISSY' WARE.

Mansion House Dwarfs A pair of grotesquely fat little figures (fig. 75) first made at Derby in 1784, copied (through a Chelsea red anchor figure) from etchings by Jacques Callot (1616). They carried advertisements on their high hats and were so named after dwarf figures that stood outside the London Mansion House similarly decorated with announcements of sales, plays etc. There are many reproductions, particularly by Samson.

Martinware (1873–1915) Art pottery made by four brothers Martin at Southall, London, chiefly vases and jugs, in saltglaze stoneware. Their most famous handiwork, made almost throughout their career, were the grotesque leering birds, resembling a cross between an owl and a vulture with a human expression, soberly coloured in brown, grey and blue; the heads are detachable (fig. 76). Quite as grotesque were many jugs modelled as clownish human faces (fig. 77). Other more conventionally shaped jugs and vases of the middle period were incised or coloured in a wider palette with designs derived from vegetable or marine life, sometimes with birds (realistic birds) or dragons. No two pieces were the same, not even the pawns of a chess set; each was signed and dated, even to the day of the month. The grotesqueries repel some, but have quadrupled in price in the last ten years; the Martins themselves were quite indifferent to profit and rejected much of their own work.

Masonic china   The establishment of the Grand Lodge of England (1717) marked the beginnings of modern Freemasonry there. Early symbols on 18th-century pottery and porcelain included the beehive (industriousness) and ladder. In addition to the square, trowel and compass (with the motto 'Keep within compass'), there came the all-seeing eye of God, the 24-in. rule (a reminder that each hour of the day must be passed honourably and charitably), and Classical columns (for stability of character). One inscription reads: 'The World is in pain our secrets to gain'.

Mason's Patent Ironstone China (1813)   Possibly because of its inspired name, the most successful of the various types of STONE CHINA, patented by C. J. Mason of Lane Delph (Staffordshire). Its most familiar form is the octagonal jug with snake handle and all-over japan patterns in shades of pale blue and red (fig. 78). Great

76 (*left*)
MARTINWARE
Love-bird group,
1914 (*Sotheby's
Belgravia*)

77 (*right*) MARTIN-
WARE Double-face
jug, orange and
ochre, 1902
(*Sotheby's Belgravia*)

78 (*below*) MASON'S
PATENT IRONSTONE
CHINA Two octagonal
jugs (*Godden of
Worthing*)

quantities of dinner and dessert services were made, very durable though very heavy. After 1848 the moulds and engravings passed to other firms and eventually to Ashworths, who have continued to use the name ever since, but have lightened the weight of the body.

Meigh family Staffordshire potters at Hanley, trading as Job Meigh & Son (c. 1805–35) and under various other styles. The 'Son', Charles, built up a large business, mainly in blue-and-white, but also painted earthenware ('opaque porcelain'), Gothic jugs in white stoneware (see APOSTLE JUGS), parian figures etc. At Shelton another Meigh traded as Hicks & Meigh etc. (1806–36), also making blue-and-white and stone china. (Pronounced mee.)

Miniature china Sets of porcelain or pottery table services, too large for the doll's house, too small for use, made as children's toys and as cabinet pieces by many firms, some in early saltglaze, tortoiseshell or pearlware. Many sets are true replicas of adult-sized wares, subsidiary items included. A 19th-century Staffordshire firm, Green & Co., specialized in them; they were also made by Rockingham, Swansea, Ridgway etc. and are still being made by Worcester and Copeland.

Minton (1793–today) A factory founded at Stoke-on-Trent, Staffordshire, by Thomas Minton, an engraver who had worked for Caughley, Wedgwood and Spode; it was greatly expanded by his son Herbert (1836–58). The range of products has been exceptionally varied and always of high quality, from the early blue-printed earthenwares (including Willow Pattern) and porcelain with New Hall-type decoration onwards. Minton's contribution to the fine porcelain

79 MINTON Flower-encrusted basket, *c.* 1830–35

of the first half of the last century has been greatly
under-rated until quite recently when research among
pattern-books etc. has shown that a great deal of it has
been wrongly attributed to Worcester, Derby,
Rockingham, Swansea, Spode and Coalport. In
particular, most of the best flower-encrusted 'COAL-
BROOKDALE' wares are now known to have come from
Minton's (1825–40; fig. 79); and quantities of figures,
busts and groups (celebrities, fictional characters,
dogs, figures designed as candle-snuffers etc.), some in
the biscuit, have been attributed to Coalport, Derby
or Rockingham but were made at Minton's (*c.* 1825–
1850). Ground colours were very varied, the most
famous being a distinctive turquoise.

From the 1840s the firm diversified into PARIAN
figures, majolica, Sèvres imitations decorated by
foreign artists, 'PALISSY' WARE and M. L. Solon's
PÂTE-SUR-PÂTE vases (1870–1904); all these were of

113

very high quality. Minton have made a point of employing first-class artists, including the Derby artists Joseph Bancroft, Thomas Steel and George Hancock, who arrived from Derby in the 1830s.

This factory's later wares, when marked, are more easily datable than most; pattern numbers were introduced early (reaching 9000 c. 1850) and since 1842 there has been a distinguishing symbol for each year; major artists also applied their own marks.

Mocha ware (c. 1780–today) Cheap colour-banded pottery, mostly mugs and jugs, decorated with fern-like designs resembling those in moss agate ('Mocha-stone', once shipped from Mocha on the Red Sea). Bands carrying the Mocha design were of alkaline slip on which, while wet, were put drops of acid 'tea', originally concocted from tobacco juice, urine or hops coloured with a metallic oxide; by capillary action, assisted by tilting the piece or by blowpipe, the 'tea' stains spread to form feathery designs, normally brown, sometimes blue or green. In early creamware specimens the bands were blue, yellow, white or brown; in late Victorian times, grey and blue. Mocha ware, invented in Staffordshire, was made all over Britain and even in France. The mugs were much used in pubs, and sometimes carry excise marks. See fig. 80.

Money-boxes As these were made to be broken open, preferably at Christmas, few survive from the 18th century, when the favourite forms were a hen on a nest-egg or the Sussex piggy-bank; some in speckled green. A group of farmer, wife and cows is another 18th-century form. Those of later date that survive

80 MOCHA WARE. Welsh jug, *c.* 1850 (*City Museum, Stoke-on-Trent*)

81 MONKEY BAND Copeland & Garrett figures (*Spode-Copeland Museum*)

were probably used, if not intended, as chimney ornaments; there are many kinds of slotted cottages, some marked 'Savings Bank', one of the commonest being flanked by a boy and girl, with faces peering from the windows. Other types include cats and dogs, perhaps in 'Rockingham' glaze, beehives, or busts. Coins, and therefore the boxes, became larger in later years.

Monkey band A set of twenty or so monkeys playing musical instruments, first modelled by Kändler at Meissen c. 1750; the story that they caricature the royal orchestra of Saxony is unlikely.

They were copied by Chelsea, Derby and, from c. 1833, by Copeland & Garrett (fig. 81), but most examples seen in shops are late German hard-paste replicas.

Moustache cups Fitted with a shaped china trough across the drinking side of the rim to keep the typically luxuriant moustache of a Victorian or Edwardian head of family out of his morning tea (fig. 82). Made by many firms, sometimes with wifely inscriptions such as 'Remember Me'.

82 MOUSTACHE CUP Made by Hammersley of Longton (*Geoffrey Godden*)

Nantgarw-Swansea (1813–20) William BILLINGSLEY, with his son-in-law Samuel Walker and financed by W. W. Young, set up a very small factory at Nantgarw, near Caerphilly, and produced a beautiful porcelain which he hoped would rival the old 18th-century soft-paste Sèvres, and on which he had been experimenting for half his life; it was exceptionally translucent and chalky white. Unfortunately it was not an economic proposition as it was too glassy to stand up to high temperatures, and kiln losses were immense. Probably no products of this first Nantgarw period have survived.

In 1814 Dillwyn, of the Cambrian Pottery, came to Billingsley's rescue, hoping to improve the Nantgarw paste at his larger and better equipped factory. Nantgarw was temporarily closed, and Billingsley and Walker transferred to Swansea.

Kiln losses, however, continued high, and Dillwyn may also have heard that Billingsley, who was hiding behind a false name, was allegedly breaking an agreement with him by revealing to Flight & Barr the secret of his new paste, made just before he came to Nantgarw. However that may have been, Dillwyn abandoned the Nantgarw formula and introduced (1816–17) three new pastes. The first, known as 'duck-egg Swansea' from its green translucency, contained bone-ash; it was most attractive, with a glaze that never crazed, but 'wasters' were still too numerous. The second was tougher, containing soapstone, and very glassy. The third (called 'trident' from its mark) was also a soapstone body, but proved unreliable and had a dull and pitted glaze. Dillwyn retired temporarily, handing over to the Bevington brothers (1817–1824), and porcelain production ceased at Swansea.

Billingsley and Walker returned to Nantgarw and, again financed by Young, resumed production, this time with an improved version of their original porcelain which had a warm white appearance and a beautiful glaze, and was even more translucent, more manageable, though still subject to uneconomic kiln losses, as indeed was the old Sèvres soft-paste porcelain which it so closely resembled. In 1820 the two partners suddenly left, leaving their personal possessions behind and without telling Young, apparently to join Rose at Coalport. Billingsley has been described as a hot-tempered man, given to horsewhipping his young employees; presumably some violent outburst preceded this extraordinary desertion.

Both factories were restricted by the nature of the pastes mainly to flatware and the smaller items of hollow-ware; figures and large jugs or vases could not survive the kiln. Tea and dessert services (Plate 2) were the chief products, together with such items as inkwells, candlesticks, spill-vases and cabinet cups and saucers mostly in French Empire shapes that appealed to Regency tastes.

Whether decorated in Wales or, as so much of it was, in London, Nantgarw and Swansea wares are alike famous for the high quality of the painting on most of them, especially the floral designs no doubt inspired by the flower-painter *par excellence*, Billingsley. At Swansea he himself painted mostly on the glassy soapstone type of porcelain, specializing in landscapes in addition to flowers; his backer, Young, was a naturalist and painted botanical and bird designs; Thomas Baxter painted gardens, landscapes and classical figures. Wildflower designs were a Swansea speciality, and several japan patterns were adopted.

Most Nantgarw and much of the duck-egg Swansea were bought in the white by London dealers whose artists decorated them lavishly in the 18th-century Sèvres style, with exotic birds, figure groups, named landscapes etc. For ten years or so after Billingsley disappeared 'production' continued, inasmuch as large stocks in the white, accumulated in London and at both factories, were being decorated and sold. At Nantgarw these were unglazed and included, unfortunately, 'seconds'; under Young's direction they were given an inferior glaze, decorated by Thomas Pardoe and sold locally. Pardoe, formerly of the Cambrian Pottery, was versatile and could turn his hand to botanical, bird, animal, landscape and even oriental themes. Swansea stocks were decorated, mainly with floral designs, by Evans, Pollard and Morris, both under the Bevington régime and after Dillwyn resumed control of the Cambrian Pottery in 1824.

Identification thus presents even more problems than usual: there were four quite different pastes; wares decorated locally and in London, in the Billingsley period and post-Billingsley; close imitations by Coalport, where Rose had probably bought the moulds of both factories and even copper plates marked 'Swansea'; and a great many fakes, English and Continental, hard and soft paste. In general, Swansea tridents if painted, 'Swansea' if painted in capital letters, and most painted 'Nantgarw' marks are suspect.

New Hall (1781–1835) A Staffordshire factory, at Hanley, which made a strikingly durable hard-paste porcelain and, from c. 1814, bone china; tea and coffee sets predominated.

The **hard paste** was based on a patent bought from Champion of Bristol but differed in appearance from Bristol (and all other) hard paste because it was differently treated in the kiln and had a lead glaze. Translucency is uneven and the body shows greyish against the light. The glaze is clear, free from crazing and imparts a candle-grease feel; gas bubbles at handle and spout joints are another aid to identification. Some wares, especially of the first decade, are of excellent quality but there was a gradual lowering of sights to suit a Midlands middle-class market.

Pieces (except cups and saucers) usually bear a boldly written pattern number, sometimes preceded by 'N' or 'No.' Among the best-known designs (from over 1000) are No. 195 (the 'sprigged muslin' decoration typical of New Hall) and No. 20 ('Boy with Kite', one of several CHINOISERIE designs with puppet-like figures). Decoration was drawn freehand at first and there were many pleasingly restrained designs with high-quality gilding (a New Hall speciality); polychrome, painted and transfer-printed blue-and-white decoration were all used.

'Typical' New Hall shapes were often based on silver counterparts, e.g. the fluted polygonal teapots (fig. 83) and helmet-shaped cream jugs; they are misleading

83 NEW HALL
Teapot, c. 1800

guides to recognition, however, as similar shapes were made in bone china by Caughley, Coalport, Minton and Chamberlain, and there are deliberate copies in hard paste by unknown factories in addition to the Caughley/Coalport hard-paste (see CAUGHLEY). Outmoded handle-less tea-bowls were still made at first, allegedly because the Midlands clientèle still drank from the saucer, which was deep but had no well.

The **bone china** was cheaper to make and much whiter; it was often decorated with the earlier patterns, new patterns being numbered from about 1050 upwards, but with an added factory mark.

Nodders   Porcelain (sometimes pottery) figures with detachable heads which oscillate, usually nodding but sometimes wagging sideways. Through the neck a pin is fixed which should be of flat metal on edge (often replaced by a round pin) resting on grooves in the shoulders. The earliest (mandarins) are rare; the commonest are blue-and-white pairs of children dressed up as elders, with metal spectacles; there are also Buddhas, animals, clowns and groups of figures (e.g. a tea-party). The best are French (possibly Limoges) or Dresden (c. 1850); most come from other German factories (including that which made FAIRINGS); others are Staffordshire. Some heads do not belong to the bodies; to get a poor nodder to nod properly is quite difficult.

Nottingham stoneware (c. 1690–1850)   A form of fine lightweight saltglazed STONEWARE with a bronze sheen (sometimes called BROWNWARE). Best-known products are the jugs in the form of a bear, with a rough coat of clay chips (fig. 84); and a fierce but unlikely lion, a foot long. Also made were very well

84 NOTTINGHAM STONEWARE Typical bear-jug (*Nottingham Castle Museum*)

designed teapots, puzzle-jugs, and 'decantors' (necked jugs) etc., some with incised or carved-out decoration.

'Palissy' ware   Minton's name for relief-decorated colour-glazed wares hardly distinguishable from their 'MAJOLICA'.   Some of it imitated the work of the 16th-century French potter Bernard Palissy, who made distinctive wares decorated with lizards and other creatures or plants in high relief and harmonious coloured lead glazes.   These were also copied at Lambeth *c.* 1650.

Pap-boat   A shallow boat-shaped vessel with a tubular spout, for feeding infants or invalids.

Parian (*c.* 1842)   Unglazed fine-grained porcelain, introduced by Copeland & Garrett as 'Statuary porcelain' and by Minton as 'Parian', named after the Ancient Greek marble from the island of Paros.   In a soft-paste form it was used to emulate early Derby biscuit figures by making copies of classical statues (especially nudes; fig. 85). These two firms were the principal producers; Wedgwood's 'Carrara' was similar. Quality ranged from excellent to sickly sentimental. Some copies of sculpture were made with a device (resembling the pantograph used to copy maps on a different scale) invented by Benjamin Cheverton; these bear his name. Wall plaques and commemorative pieces were also made.

A different, cheaper, hard-paste form was introduced a few years later for moulded and glazed jugs, hand-vases etc. This proved to be easily soiled and difficult to clean. GOSS is a variety.

Pâte-sur-pâte (*c.* 1870) A very elaborate and expensive method of relief decoration introduced at the Minton factory (from Sèvres) by M. L. Solon, who signed his work (fig. 86). The typical form was a tall classical urn with reliefs built up by thin coats of white slip laboriously applied one on top of another on an

85 PARIAN
Minton figure of
Mercury, *c.* 1850
(*Victoria and
Albert Museum*)

123

unfired but coloured parian body, to produce cameo-like designs of cupids etc. against a dark background. The rough result was then tooled into shape and glazed. This technique was imitated by Grainger's Worcester, Royal Worcester, Doulton and others.

Pearlware (1779) A white, harder, more durable form of QUEEN'S WARE, also produced by Wedgwood; it was said to contain a higher proportion of pipeclay and flint, and the glaze was blued with a touch of cobalt. Wedgwood pearlware was marked 'Pearl' from 1840 and 'P' from 1868. Leeds (fig. 65) and other potters also made it.

Pinxton (1796–1813) A Derbyshire factory near Mansfield founded by John Coke urged on by BILLINGS-LEY (who was then at Derby). For a brief period before one of Billingsley's periodic desertions (1799), the factory was able to make a porcelain resembling the finest he later made at NANTGARW-SWANSEA, though equally uneconomic. For the rest, the pro-ducts, almost exclusively useful wares, resembled Derby in paste and decoration, the latter notable for landscape vignettes (fig. 87) in monochrome or colours, floral designs naturally excellent under Billingsley's influence, and first-class gilding; coloured grounds were less successful. Pinxton is rather scarce and rarely marked.

Plymouth (c. 1768–70) The earliest English hard-paste porcelain factory, founded by William Cook-worthy who had been trying since the 1740s to dis-cover the right materials to imitate Chinese porcelain. Finding them at last in Cornwall, he took out a patent which gave him the monopoly of their exploitation and set up a factory in near-by Plymouth. This

proved too remote and he moved to Bristol, but handed over to Richard Champion *c.* 1773 (see CHAMPION'S BRISTOL). It is more useful to classify their products as Cookworthy's (1768–73) and Champion's (1773–1781) than as Plymouth and Bristol, since those made

under Cookworthy's management at Bristol are indistinguishable from Plymouth.

Cookworthy's paste was not a success. It had to be
fired at a higher temperature than Chinese or Continental porcelain. It tended to be discoloured by the
smoke of wood fuel, and was prone to warping in the
kiln, bubbled and flecked surfaces, firecracks etc.
Wares thrown on the wheel were purposely
'wreathed' (i.e. potted in varying thicknesses) to
lessen the danger of kiln collapse. Most products
were painted in an inky underglaze blue with floral
or Chinese themes, or enamelled with flowers, exotic
birds in landscapes etc.; the enamels often flaked and
colours were sometimes spoilt by overfiring. Straight-
sided or bell-shaped mugs were very popular; also
silver-shaped sauceboats. Perhaps the most successful
pieces were the well decorated hexagonal vases
(fig. 88; discontinued by Champion). A few figures

(Seasons, Continents etc.), mostly copying Longton Hall models, were made, with rococo bases; the latest ones are marked 'To' (see TEBO) and may have been modelled by the Derby craftsman Pierre Stéphan. Animal and bird figures were also made.

Portobello (*c.* 1786) A seaside town, now part of Edinburgh, with several potteries which traded under various names. The Scott Brothers (*c.* 1786–96) made green-glaze wares and possibly brown earthenware transfer-printed in yellow.

To a pottery owned (*c.* 1808–37) by Thomas Rathbone and his son are attributed a series of rather primitive but attractive figures on round bases, notably fishwives (fig. 89), soldiers and sailors; also lions, domestic animals and birds in early Prattware colouring. Attributions to Portobello and PRESTONPANS are largely guesswork, and these potteries passed through various hands until well into the 20th century.

Posset pots and caudle cups Two-handled lidded pots for hot drinks. The posset pot dates from at least the 17th century (see SLIPWARE) and contained hot spiced milk curdled with ale or wine, apparently a kill-or-cure for colds. Originally it had a spout, and might bear the owner's name. See fig. 90.

90 POSSET POT Bristol delftware, *c.* 1720

127

Caudle cups replaced them in favour *c.* 1750, and differed from them in having a saucer but no spout. They were made in elaborately decorated porcelain, specifically for presents to women who had just had a baby. Caudle (contracted from the Latin for 'hot') was a thin hot gruel, sweetened, spiced and laced with wine or even spirits, a pick-me-up for nursing mothers and invalids. See FOOD-WARMERS.

After *c.* 1850 they continued to be made as cabinet pieces. Some chocolate cups were made in the same style.

Pot-lids Small circular earthenware lids decorated with underglaze multi-colour transfer prints, made in Staffordshire, mostly by F. & R. Pratt of Fenton (*c.* 1847–88) but also by Mayer and related firms at Dale Hall (Longport) and possibly at the Cauldon pottery, Stoke. They covered shallow pots of bear's grease (hair pomade), fish or meat pastes, face cream etc. See PRATTWARE, LATE.

The copperplate originals of many Pratt designs were skilfully engraved by Jesse Austin, whose name or initials appear on some lids. He used one plate for the outline and others for each of the colours (yellow, blue, red), accuracy of registration being ensured by dots, which may be seen on either side of the finished product.

There were about 600 designs, including bear motifs, scenes at Pegwell Bay (Kentish fishing and shrimping centre), the Great Exhibition, portraits, Old England, sports and pastimes, animals, flowers and landscapes (Plate 6).

Brilliance of colour is the distinguishing feature of the early lids, together with fine crazing under the glaze, caused during firing. Many early lids are flat-topped, later ones rounded. There are numerous reproductions, many marked as such on the back.

Potteries, The   The six Staffordshire towns (Arnold Bennett's 'Five Towns') since 1910 comprising the borough of Stoke-on-Trent, adjacent to and east of the M6.   From north to south they are: Tunstall, Burslem with Cobridge, Hanley with Shelton, Stoke, Fenton and Longton with Lane End and Lane Delph.

Prattware, Early (c. 1780–1835)   A generic term for earthenware crudely decorated in a distinctive range of underglaze colours, with ochre, blue and green predominant; the other colours are yellow, purple-brown, grey-brown and black.   These had to withstand high temperatures as they were painted or sponged on to the body, which was then fired, finished with lead glaze and refired.   Usually the colours were applied over high-relief moulding.

Prattware is named after, and was possibly first produced by, William Pratt (1753–99) of Lane Delph (Staffordshire), grandfather of the Felix Pratt who made POT-LIDS (and see next entry).   It was also, however, made by many other potters not only in Staffordshire but in Yorkshire, Sunderland and Scotland.   The wares most often seen are jugs (Plate 2), tea-caddies, plaques and cottages (flanked by two figures).   These bear moulded designs, the commonest being celebrities (e.g. Nelson); groups such as 'The Leek Loyal Volunteers'; grotesque caricatures of bewigged men; hunting scenes etc.   There were also single figures and groups, some very crudely modelled and decorated with haphazard spots of colour, Toby jugs, cow-creamers, watchstands and teapots (of CASTLEFORD shape).

Prattware, Late (*c.* 1847–88)   A generic term for wares, especially dessert and tea services and jugs, made by F. & R. Pratt of Fenton (Staffordshire), a firm founded by Felix (1780–1859), son of William Pratt (see last entry), and carried on by Felix's son, Felix Edwards Pratt (1813–94), who developed the colour printing process used in POT-LIDS. These tablewares were decorated by the same process and are notable for their borders in malachite green (fig. 91; particularly prized), red, pink, blue or maroon; another favourite border had an intricate oak-leaf design.

Prestonpans   A town near Edinburgh which had two potteries making similar wares: Gordon's (*c.* 1750–1832) and Watson's (*c.* 1750–1840).   Watson's may have made the stiffly posed earthenware figures of fish-wives often attributed to PORTOBELLO, and a set of Scottish national heroes; Gordon's may have made early Prattware.   Other attributions are wares similar to Goss and Belleek, flatbacks, majolica and tiles.   In 1900 a later pottery there became the Scottish Porcelain Co.

Punch-bowl   A large bowl, made in most kinds of pottery and porcelain, often lustreware transfer-printed in black with hunting, shipping or political themes (fig. 93).   Originally an Indian drink of five (Hindi *punch*) ingredients, including arrack (fermented coconut milk etc.) and tea, punch was transformed in England into a spiced and sweetened mixture of brandy, rum or wine with fruit juices, usually served hot.

Puzzle jugs   Jugs (fig. 92) from which it is impossible to drink unless one knows the trick.   Typic-

91 (*right*) PRATTWARE, LATE 'Hop Queen' plate with malachite border (*Sotheby's Belgravia*)

92 (*left*) PUZZLE JUGS Staffordshire scratch blue jug, 1764 (*Victoria and Albert Museum*)

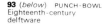

93 (*below*) PUNCH-BOWL Eighteenth-century delftware

ally there is a hollow handle (sometimes with a hole in it) leading to a tube round the rim connecting three or more spouts; drink can be sucked through one of these if all other apertures are stopped. Such jugs were made from *c.* 1570 until the early 1800s, in delftware, brown saltglaze, creamware etc. Some kinds, to make things more difficult, had openwork decoration round the jug below the spouts.

Queen's Ware (1765) The name given by Josiah Wedgwood to his improved CREAMWARE after Queen Charlotte had bought some; it captured the market, at home and overseas. The name was borrowed by many other Staffordshire potters. See PEARLWARE.

Railway themes The sudden transition to mechanical transport is vividly commemorated by a Minton mask-jug (1847) contrasting stage-coach and rail travel. Other pottery jugs, mugs and plates depict such scenes as the inauguration of the Liverpool-Manchester line (1830), one showing the Duke of Wellington in the front seat of a carriage, doubtless deafened by a band in the adjacent truck; George

94 RAILWAY THEMES George Stephenson driving his latest model at the opening of the Liverpool—Manchester Railway. 1830

Stephenson (fig. 94) driving one of his locomotives (1832); the 'Rocket', viaducts, railway stations etc., all transfer-printed.

Redware   Red stoneware, usually unglazed and often decorated with applied motifs in relief.   The term includes ELERS WARE and similar products; the harder, polished 'red china' patented (1729) by Samuel Bell of Newcastle; and the more attractively coloured 'rosso antico' of Wedgwood (1760s).   Highly polished red stoneware was also used as a base for copper lustre.

Ridgways   A family of Staffordshire potters chiefly associated, in a series of shifting partnerships, with two Shelton (Hanley) potteries: Bell Works (1792) and Cauldon Place (1802).   The brothers Job and George were partners at the former until Job founded the latter, where he was joined by his sons John and William (who traded as John & William Ridgway, 1814–30).   Then until c. 1855 William ran the Bell Works and John Cauldon Place, the latter passing by stages into the ownership of Brown-Westhead, Moore (1862) and then to Cauldon Ltd (1905).

Both potteries produced high-quality useful wares in porcelain (fig. 95), earthenware and stoneware, especially tea and dessert services.   The porcelain of the 1802–40 period was rarely marked and its technical and artistic standards (particularly the floral and landscape painting) have led to much of it being attributed to Worcester, Rockingham or Spode, as has been shown by recent study of pattern books and numbers. The range included splendidly elaborate tureens, fruit baskets and two-handled dessert dishes of the 1810–20 period.

Notable among the pottery are: stone china with named patterns, and printed earthenware in pale blue and fine detail (John and William at Cauldon); and near-white stoneware jugs with detailed scenes modelled in high relief (William at Bell).

Rockingham A name normally reserved for the fine and usually lavishly decorated porcelain (bone china) produced (*c.* 1826–42) at Swinton, near Doncaster, but also applicable to pottery (see below), which was first made there *c.* 1745. The factory was taken over by the Brameld family (1806), who began to make porcelain commercially about 1826. The site was on the Marquess of Rockingham's estate, which passed to his nephew, Earl Fitzwilliam, in 1782; the latter took great personal interest in the firm and rescued it from bankruptcy several times.

Rockingham's reputation was chiefly due to Thomas Brameld, a man of great taste who relied (unduly, it seems) on profits from pottery to subsidize losses on porcelain; and to his brother John, who decorated some of the products. Their market was primarily the aristocracy, particularly after the completion (1830) for William IV of a magnificent dessert service, still used at Buckingham Palace.

In potting, glaze and decoration Rockingham was probably the best of its time. The griffin mark (from the Fitzwilliam crest) was at first red and after 1830 puce. The *Red Griffin porcelain* was finer, shapes and decoration simpler; the outstanding feature was the fine coloured grounds in shades of blue, green or red, often with reserved panels painted with romantic scenes and surrounded by elaborate gilding. The *Puce Griffin porcelain* followed the revived vogue for rococo; shapes were more elaborate (e.g. handles

95 (*right*) RIDGWAYS Plate, John Ridgway & Bates, *c.* 1857 (*Victoria and Albert Museum*)

96 (*left*) ROCKINGHAM Cabinet cup and saucer

97 (*right*) ROCKINGHAM Typical piece of the Puce Griffin period, 1830–42 (*Rotherham Museum*)

with one or three spurs); grounds were less colourful—grey or green surrounded by distinctive gilt lacework scrolls; great use was made of small applied flowers.

Tea (figs. 96 and 97) and dessert services were the chief wares throughout; spill-vases and hexagonal vases were particularly attractive. Figures were probably made only in the earlier period, some biscuit, some coloured, modelled in clear detail and standing on plinths. Human figures included theatrical, rural and child subjects and a series of named 'foreign peasants'; poodles and sheep have smooth coats. All these are marked; there is no evidence that the traditional 'Rockingham' animals with rough coats of shredded china come from Rockingham, and the same applies to 'Rockingham' flower-encrusted cottages.

Contrary to tradition, true Rockingham is relatively scarce and most of it is marked, except that in services the griffin appears, in general, only on plates and saucers; but painted pattern numbers (between 545 and 1559) on the unmarked pieces assist identification, and shapes are often distinctive, as is a fine, barely visible, crazing. Cabinet pieces often bear a gilder's mark (Cl. 1–14). Much 'Rockingham' is now known to be Coalport (especially wares encrusted with larger flowers than Rockingham used), Bloor Derby, Davenport, Copeland etc.; excessively rococo designs are never Rockingham but may be Coalport, Grainger's Worcester or Samuel Alcock. Pieces marked with the griffin and 'Brameld' were made in London (1842–1854) by J. W. Brameld.

As to **pottery**, little is known of the coarse brown earthenware made at Swinton until 1765. From 1778 a thick manganese brown 'Rockingham glaze' was used on hard earthenware CADOGANS, Toby jugs, coffee-

98 (near right)
ROYAL
WORCESTER
PORCELAIN CO.
Highland sheep
painted by Harry
Davis, 1901
(Sotheby's
Belgravia)

99 (far right)
ROYAL
WORCESTER
PORCELAIN CO.
'Irish Navvy'.
1912. (Mary
Payton Antiques)

pots etc., and continued until the 1820s; also a green glaze on creamware. Swinton was once (1787–1806) controlled by Leeds and made creamware. Transfer-printed wares in blue or other colours and earthenware hand-painted with naturalistic flowers are marked 'Brameld', later 'Rockingham'.

Rogers family Staffordshire potters at Longport from c. 1784. John Rogers & Son (1815–36) were prolific producers of blue-and-white wares, mostly marked, decorated with series of Oriental and Classical themes, 'The Drama'—scenes from popular plays and operas with details on the back—and many other designs.

Royal Worcester Porcelain Co. (1862–today) Founded by R. W. Binns (see CHAMBERLAIN'S WORCESTER), this factory was first notable for ivory-tinted porcelain decorated in popular Japanese styles, including vases carved in deep relief by James Hadley. This versatile artist also modelled a series of Kate Greenaway children. He set up on his own in 1875 but the firm bought all his work until 1896, when he and his sons began making 'Hadley ware'—vases with coloured clay embellishments and floral designs, which the firm continued to make after his death in 1903. Many biscuit figures were made with painted details; others in cream shading into dark brown (fig. 99). There was also a delightful series nicknamed 'Down-and-outs'—men in battered headgear; intended for use as menu-holders.

The other main product was expensive tableware etc. decorated with tinted gold and other metallic colours. From just before the turn of the century the firm employed many notable artists, e.g. Harry Davis (fig. 98; landscapes and sheep), C. H. C. Baldwyn (birds, swans etc.) and John Stinton (landscapes, cattle, sheep); the last had previously worked for Grainger.

Saltglaze (c. 1720–80) Staffordshire white STONE-WARE glazed by throwing rock-salt into the kiln at peak temperature; the volatilized salt combined with the silicon and aluminium oxides in the clay to form a pitted 'orange-peel' surface. The white body was developed from earlier brown stoneware (also salt-glazed) by using Devon pipeclay mixed with calcined flint; it appears to have been originated c. 1671 by John Dwight of Fulham and adopted in Staffordshire shortly afterwards by one of the Astburys (perhaps John; see ASTBURY WARE) and by others.

Among the wares so made were loving-cups (fig. 72), mugs, bowls, plates, numerous teapots shaped as houses, camels etc., jugs in the shape of an owl or of a bear hugging a terrier (the heads being detachable as cups). There was a wide range of decoration—moulded, applied relief, incised (including SCRATCH BLUE), perforated, AGATE WARE, and eventually overglaze enamels; some pieces were left undecorated.

Most interesting was the quaintly amusing series of small hand-modelled figures and groups attributed to Astbury, Aaron Wood (1717–85) and others, especially the oddly named *pew-groups* (1730–40). In these, two or three pop-eyed persons sit stiffly on a high-backed bench engaged in flirtation or playing improbable musical instruments; details are picked out in dark brown clay. In similar style are the 'arbour groups' (lovers seated under a crudely modelled tree, forerunner of the WALTON bocage); horsemen holding charmingly rigid postures as if struck by lightning (fig. 100); a bell shaped like a woman; an Adam and Eve group; birds, dogs, cats etc.

These saltglaze stoneware figures have a family resemblance to the earthenware figures made contemporaneously (and sometimes by the same potters)

100 SALTGLAZE Staffordshire figure, details picked out in brown clay. *c.* 1730 (*Victoria and Albert Museum*)

which are classified as ASTBURY, ASTBURY-WHIELDON or WHIELDON. Both kinds command very high prices and are not often seen outside museums; they have however been faked. Those made in the 1730s and 1740s were unsophisticated products of native Staffordshire humour and ante-date even the earliest English porcelain figures; but by the 1750s William Duesbury and others were using this perhaps inappropriate medium for enamel-painted imitations of Meissen and Chinese themes.

Scent bottles The magnificent 'Chelsea toys' have been mentioned under CHELSEA and GIRL-IN-A-SWING FACTORY. Other 18th-century bottles were made at Derby and in saltglaze, agate ware etc.; Wedgwood later made them in jasper. The early examples were used more as 'smelling bottles', i.e. vinaigrettes with an ornamental grille holding in a sponge steeped in aromatic vinegar ('smelling salts'), important amid the all too pervasive stenches of that epoch and also as a cure for 'the vapours', common enough when women had 14-in. waists. Early Chelsea bottles might have a patch-box at the other end, ornately decorated even internally. There were flower-encrusted examples and some double-ended Victorian types in porcelain (handkerchief scent at one end, smelling salts at the other). Accurate copies of birds' eggs in pottery were another popular form from the 1850s.

Scratch blue A form of SGRAFFITO WARE in which the incisions are filled in with cobalt blue pigment. This decoration is found on early SALTGLAZE, especially on dated and named loving-cups (fig. 72), and revived in the 1870s by DOULTONS, where Hannah Barlow was famous for her animal studies incised on jugs etc.

101 SHERRATT, OBADIAH Ale-bench group 'Tee Total', c. 1820 (*Willett Collection, Brighton*)

Sgraffito ware A form of SLIPWARE (also called sgraffiato or scratch ware) in which the coating of slip is scratched away to produce patterns in the contrasting colour of the underlying body; the scratching is done before glazing. Sgraffito has a long history but in England is chiefly associated with 18th-century Staffordshire mugs and jugs decorated with animals, birds, fish etc., and with a revival at art potteries more recently. SCRATCH BLUE is one variant.

Shaving mug A lipped mug partly covered with a perforated soap-dish; the brush was wetted in the hot water through the remaining aperture and the soap lathered with it *in situ*. Made from the 1840s, they were sometimes quite decorative.

Sherratt, Obadiah (worked c. 1815–40) A Burslem (Staffordshire) potter whose crude figure groups usually differed sharply in theme and appearance from those of the WALTON SCHOOL. The best-known is the much copied group (*c.* 1830) of a man urging on his dog to bait a bull; like most of his work it is illiterately captioned—'Bull-beating. Now Captin lad'. 'Death of Monrow' celebrates the killing of a Lt. Monroe in a Bengal tiger hunt; the vast animal biting off the head of the toy-like officer (in full dress uniform) is no less realistic than that labelled 'Roran [roaring] lion'. A more ambitious group (*c.* 1814) is 'Polito's Menagerie'. Isaac's near-sacrifice is labelled 'Abram stop', *tout court*. Domesticities are dealt with in two 'Ale-bench' groups (fig. 101) in which a wife forcibly converts her husband to teetotalism, and in 'Who shall ware the Breches'. Most of these groups are on rickety-looking four- or six-legged bases.

Slipware Earthenware decorated with white or coloured slip, i.e. clay mixed with water to a creamy consistency. The slip was used in various ways: as an overall coating; trailed over the pottery much as cakes are iced (fig. 40); or as applied moulded decoration. Slipware was usually given a yellowish lead glaze.

There are Roman-British, Persian, Byzantine-Venetian and English pre-Reformation examples. The art was revived early in the 17th century at Wrotham (Kent; pronounced root'em), where they made ornate tygs (mugs with more than one handle, for passing round at convivial gatherings; fig. 102) and lidded POSSET POTS. Similar wares were made in Staffordshire and the West Country.

Best known are dishes (*c.* 1670–85) with Thomas Toft's name prominently trailed in slip on the rim; these bore extraordinarily child-like and attractive designs such as Charles II conspicuously hiding in his oak-tree, the heraldic pelican 'in her piety', a mermaid, or Adam and Eve (a theme taken from delft-

102 SLIPWARE
Wrotham tyg

ware). Various forms of slipware were still being made by country potters in the 19th century, notably the striped 'Welsh ware' meat dishes with zig-zag patterns. See also SGRAFFITO WARE.

Spode (1770–today) A Staffordshire firm established at Stoke-on-Trent by the Spode family and continued from 1833 by the Copeland family in whose hands it remained until recently (it is now American-owned); famous for bone china and BLUE-AND-WHITE wares. Josiah Spode I, who had been apprenticed to Whieldon, ran the firm until his death (1797), making fine stoneware, creamware, BLACK BASALT, lustre-ware and other types of pottery, introducing to Staffordshire TRANSFER-PRINTING in underglaze blue (c. 1781) and marketing (c. 1794) bone china (see Introduction, page 16), the invention of which is traditionally attributed to his son and successor, Josiah II.

Josiah II (1797–1827) introduced 'New STONE CHINA' (c. 1805), probably the best of its kind. This was intended for the cheaper market; for the gentry 'Felspar porcelain' was made (c. 1815–33; see Introduction, page 16). Henry Daniel was the chief

143

the figures emanating from the WALTON SCHOOL (c. 1806–46), with their distinctive green BOCAGES and typically high roundish bases (instead of the square bases hitherto in favour). Divorced from all these traditions were the works (c. 1815–40) of an illiterate individualist, Obadiah SHERRATT, who revelled in sudden death and the sex war.

It is, however, surprising that so much sweetness and light should have emerged from the insanitary shacks in which so many of these figures were made. With drunkenness and absenteeism rife among their elders, much of the work must have fallen to the children; as recently as 1842 an official report recorded the case of a boy of 9 producing 40 dozen small figures each day of a 6-day week—at 4d. a day. See also next entry.

Staffordshire figures, Victorian Three years after coming to the throne in 1837 Queen Victoria married Prince Albert. This event coincided with an outburst of activity in the making of figures in a new tradition, most of them portrait figures and commemorating current events, in the fields of war, sport, crime, entertainment (fig. 103) and religion; but first came the Royal Family (Plate 1). In addition vast quantities of 'china' dogs were made, the most familiar being the soulful-looking spaniel which gazes out of most antique-shop windows and which, after the first shock, tends to grow on one.

These figures were no longer hand-modelled but moulded on bold simplified lines in very white earthenware; skilful design cut costs by reducing the number of mould-sections to two or three. Decoration was characterized for the first 20 years by a brilliant underglaze blue (especially handy for uniforms), to which

was added further embellishment in bright overglaze
enamels and gilt. As the years went by decoration
was simplified until by the late 1860s it was usually a
matter of black and white with a touch of gilt.
Realizing that these figures would grace not the dining-
table but the mantelpiece, and would thus be viewed
from the front only, the potters gradually stopped
colouring or moulding the back, thus producing the
familiar Victorian *flat-back*.

Mounted figures were vastly popular. The diminu-
tive horses look as if they were sired by rocking-horses
on circus ponies; their be-uniformed riders gaze
stiffly sideways at the onlooker as if defying impudent
criticism, and in the end the critical may well succumb
to their primitive charm, the effect having been
likened to that of the works of the Douanier Rousseau.

The portrait figures were often named on the base,
but as likenesses were usually perfunctory, it was
simple to switch titles. Queen Victoria suffered
this indignity at the commencement of her reign;

overwhelmed by public demand, the potters took the figure of an actress, stuck a crown on her head, and labelled it 'Her Majesty Queen Victoria'.

In the first few years of the 1840s there were already, in addition to royalties, figures commemorating personalities in cricket (see CRICKET THEMES), crime, the circus; the 'Railway King' who made a dubious fortune out of railways; Grace Darling, the lighthouse-keeper's daughter who helped rescue passengers from a wreck; and Afghan war heroes. Thomas Balston has noted the Radical and Nonconformist bias of the potters, allied to intense patriotism and loyalty to the throne. Tories are vitually ignored in favour of Peel and Cobden (Repeal of the Corn Laws, 1846), Gladstone etc.; Wesley, Sankey and Moody are commemorated and 'No Popery' themes of 1851, but no archbishops; Garibaldi, but Napoleon Bonaparte only as a character in a play; Napoleon III is welcomed as an ally in the Crimean War (1854) but shown prone under the British Lion, during an invasion scare, six years later. Wars, in particular, stimulated production—whether the Indian Mutiny (Colin Campbell, Highland Jessie), Crimean War (Florence Nightingale), American Civil War (John Brown, Uncle Tom, Lincoln) or the Franco-Prussian War (1870), in which Staffordshire sympathies swung from Germany to France. Byron, Scott, Burns (with or without Highland Mary) are among those representing literature, and Sir John Franklin the explorers.

Two interesting series of figures have been distinguished, well modelled and decorated all round. The factories that made them are unknown, but they are so well done that until recently they were often called 'Rockingham', although not porcelain. One, given the name '*Alpha factory*', in the period c. 1845–51 produced figures with titles usually in impressed capitals. The other was called the *Tallis factory* (c. 1849–67) because the figures first noticed were copied from engravings in Tallis's *Shakespeare Gallery*. They differ from the Alpha figures in being very heavy, having no underglaze blue, and sometimes in having transfer-printed titles. The Tallis and many other early Victorian moulds came into the hands of *William Kent* (1885 onwards) and eventually William Kent (Porcelains) Ltd., who used them until 1962. Pugh suggests that they may have been made by *Thomas Parr* of Burslem (worked 1852–70) and then passed to Kent & Parr (1880–94). The many reproductions of Victorian figures are usually referred to as 'Kent copies'; colouring, in which iron-red predominates, is crudely done and the indented titles clumsily filled in with black. Many of the flatbacks, which flourished particularly in the 1850s, were made by *Sampson Smith* of Longton (c. 1846–78); his name and moulds were used by successor firms until 1963. Some flatbacks were made elsewhere in Staffordshire, and in Scotland (Portobello, Prestonpans).

Figures decorated in underglaze blue were made before c. 1863; those gilded with a hard, unattractive 'bright gold' after c. 1880; those without crazing are probably modern (some crazing is faked, but clumsily). Reproductions lack lead glaze (which is now illegal), are less finely painted in colours a shade too vivid, and are either heavier or much lighter than the originals. The lighter ones are slip-cast instead of moulded, as is indicated by the thin potting and smooth interior finish (usually only available for inspection in broken pieces). The most notorious fakes are of Grace

Darling, Shylock, Turpin and the ubiquitous group (originally 1860) in which the bruisers Heenan and Sayers land simultaneous straight lefts while gazing at the public (fig. 104).

Staffordshire groups The theme of some often-seen pottery groups may need a little explanation:

The Tithe Pig Group (c. 1770; Plate 1) This, alone of the groups mentioned here, was originally a porcelain (Derby) group, but was widely copied by Walton and others. A farmer's wife offers to pay a shocked parson his tithe with her tenth child instead of the pig held by her husband. This parson reappears on a Toby jug inscribed 'I will have no child tho the X pig'.

The Vicar and Moses (attributed to Ralph Wood I, c. 1770) The vicar is asleep in a two-decker pulpit; the parish clerk in the lower deck reads the sermon (fig. 105).

The Parson and Clerk (attributed to Enoch Wood, c. 1790) A drunk parson is escorted home by lantern light; said to be inspired by a newspaper item about a parson who at his death left very few books but quantities of wine.

The Marriage Act A parson marries a couple in the presence of his clerk. A notice reads 'The New Marriage Act', gives the names of the couple and adds 'That is right says the parson amen says the clerk'. This refers to an Act of 1822 (partly repealed next year) regarding the validity of 'informal' marriages.

See also SHERRATT, OBADIAH.

Stirrup-cup As this was handed to people in the saddle, to fortify them at meets, it did not have to stand up and could take any fanciful shape, usually an animal's head—fox, deer, hare, fish, many kinds of

104 (*top left*) STAFFORDSHIRE
FIGURES, VICTORIAN Heenan and
Sayers; late copy of 1860 group
(*Sotheby's Belgravia*)

105 (*top right*) STAFFORDSHIRE
GROUPS The Vicar and Moses,
Ralph Wood, *c.* 1770 (*City
Museum, Stoke-on-Trent*)

106 (*above left*) STIRRUP-CUP
(*Willett Collection, Brighton*)

107 (*right*) STONEWARE 'Reform'
flask inscribed 'Grey's Reform
Cordial' and 'The People's Rights';
by Bourne of Belper and Denby,
c. 1834 (*Derby Museum*)

dog (fig. 106). It was an Ancient Greek idea, and their name for it, *rhyton*, is used in catalogues. They were made in porcelain or pottery.

Stone china A form of heavy earthenware made with felspar, resembling porcelain in outward appearance and 'ring', but cheaper to make; first patented (1800) by the Turner brothers of Lane End, Staffordshire. Josiah Spode II bought the rights (1805) and made a very dense and durable variety, marked 'Stone China' or 'New Stone'. MASON'S PATENT IRONSTONE CHINA (1813) is similar. Eventually most other potters made 'ironstone' or 'granite' china services, often decorated with japan patterns or blue-and-white transfer prints.

Stoneware Earthenware relatively rich in vitreous (glassy) material and fired at so high a temperature (about 1300°C) that it becomes as hard as stone and non-porous; one kind has long been familiar in the form of drainpipes. At FULHAM John Dwight produced BROWNWARE and REDWARE before he developed white SALTGLAZE stoneware; brown saltglaze was also made at NOTTINGHAM. From the late 1600s Lambeth and Fulham produced characteristic saltglaze jugs in two colours, dark brown above, buff below; also buff and brown spirit flasks shaped as figures (contemporary celebrities, Mrs Caudle etc.), which were made by Doulton until the glass tax was lifted (1845). 'Reform' flasks (fig. 107), made by Bourne of Denby among others, celebrated the Reform Bill (1832). See also BLACK BASALT; BELLARMINES; CASTLEFORD; ELERS WARE; JASPER WARE.

Studio pottery Stoneware or earthenware individually designed and made by one potter or a small

108 (*above*) STUDIO POTTERY
Stoneware vase by Bernard Leach,
1964 (*Mr and Mrs Godden Collection*)

109 (*above*) STUDIO POTTERY
Flambé vase by Bernard
Moore, *c.* 1905 (*City Museum,
Stoke-on-Trent*)

team. The Studio Pottery movement gathered
strength in the 20th century and is still flourishing.
Its origins may be traced back to William DE MORGAN,
MARTINWARE, the Barlows' work at DOULTONS,
CASTLE HEDINGHAM, DELLA ROBBIA WARE, WEMYSS
WARE, LINTHORPE POTTERY etc. The greatest of the
moderns has been Bernard Leach who, after studying
pottery in Japan, set up his studio in St Ives, Cornwall
(1920), and recruited his four sons to assist (fig. 108).

William Moorcroft, who worked at Burslem
(1913–45) and was succeeded by his son, experimented
with Chinese-type glazes (e.g. powder blue and
flambé) on pottery decorated with fruit and foliage in
raised outline. Somewhat similar work was done by
Bernard Moore (died 1935; fig. 109).

Sunderland There have been 16 potteries in the
neighbourhood of this Durham town, some going
back to the early 18th century. Most of them made
LUSTREWARE, especially of the splashed-pink type

(fig. 110). Other common features were transfer-prints in black, often on seafaring themes, or of the Wearmouth bridge, the longest single-span cast-iron bridge when built in 1796 (fig. 111); commemorative wares, including named and dated christening mugs and frog-mugs, usually in creamware; and WALL PLAQUES. Many pieces have verses or other inscriptions in black.

The best-known is the Garrison Pottery (1803–65), associated with the names of Dixon and Austin. They (and others) made teawares painted with child-like pictures of cottages; and many figures—Elijah, a set of Seasons, Queen Victoria, Nelson, greyhounds, 'china' dogs and 'rude' chamber-pots. The engraved copper plates passed to the Ball Brothers (of Deptford, Sunderland; 1865–1918) but they used them for coloured, not black, transfers, and their lustre was orange.

The Southwick pottery (1788–1897), associated with the Scott family but not, apparently, with the PORTOBELLO Scotts, made the Sunderland lion (as did others), heavy dinner services in sombre colours but dainty tea services gaily coloured; also jasper and Queen's wares.

These wares are often marked 'Sunderland', but so, unfortunately, are the very numerous copies.

Swansea porcelain See NANTGARW-SWANSEA.

Tea and coffee sets In the 18th century the two sets were integrated, the same saucers serving tea-cups (or bowls) and coffee cups (Plate 5). Coffee cans (which were straight-sided and had no foot-rim) were also made, mainly c. 1800–20. Apart from the teapot and its stand, there would normally be a covered *sucrier* (sugar dish) on a plate, covered cream-jug (the

110 (*left*)
SUNDERLAND Pink
lustre transfer-printed
jug, *c.* 1813–30
(*Sunderland
Museum*)

111 (*below left and
right*) SUNDERLAND
Jug decorated with
pink lustre, transfers
and underglaze
colour, showing
Wearmouth Bridge
and dedicatory verse,
1836 (*Sunderland
Museum*)

112 (*right*) TEA
AND COFFEE SETS
Spoon-tray,
'Fisherman'
pattern,
Worcester Flight/
Davis period,
1773–83 (*Mary
Payton Antiques*)

cover is now usually missing), slop basin, spoon-tray (fig. 112), possibly a *tazza* (a cake-plate rather like a COMFIT-HOLDER) and bread-and-butter plate. Individual plates were not introduced until the 1830s. Early teapots were very small, tea being so expensive (even when smuggled, as it often was) that in some quarters the used tea-leaves were spread on bread-and-butter, sugared and eaten. There was a magic about tea which, Pepys was told, was good for the defluxions (whatever they may have been); generals took it into battle.

Handle-less tea-bowls in the Chinese style were used at first (New Hall went on making them after the turn of the century). The tea was poured from the bowl to the (deep) saucer from which it was sipped, and the spoon was put on the spoon-tray; in the early 1800s a cup-plate was provided to put the cup on. The aged and ague-stricken (malaria was common) might drink safely from a two-handled *trembleuse* cup which fitted into a gallery in the saucer. Tea for one or up to four people might be served on a *cabaret* (French for, *inter alia*, a tea-tray or tea service), a porcelain tray possibly with wells for the pieces which, to economize space, were tall and waisted down to narrow bases.

113 TEA AND COFFEE SETS
Lowestoft tea-caddy

The tea-caddy was usually wooden, but Worcester supplied a tall ovoid 'teapoy' (properly the name of a small table whose only link with tea lay in the spelling) or a wider 'canister'. There were also tea-caddies in Elers or delftware and, later, in Pratt colouring; these took the flat whisky-flask shape originated by the Chinese (fig. 113).

Afternoon tea did not become fashionable until near 1800; the main tea-drinking occasion was immediately after dinner.

'Tebo, Mr' An elusive figure who drifts through the history of 18th-century English porcelain, leaving his mark ('T' or 'To') on figures and other technically complex pieces made (1750–75) at Bow, Plymouth, Bristol and Worcester as their 'repairer' (i.e. assembler; see FIGURES). Then Wedgwood employed 'Mr Tebo', as he called him, for a brief period as modeller, but he found him tiresome and (therefore?) incompetent. He was probably a Frenchman named Thibault or Thibaud, but so little is known that one writer in despair suggested that 'To' means 'top of the oven'.

Terracotta Wedgwood revived the name, particularly associated with Ancient Greek pottery including the 4th-century B.C. Tanagra statuettes, for the unglazed porous earthenwares, usually red, in which he made classical-shaped vases. Later, terracotta wares were made by Minton, Copeland, F. & R. Pratt and many others. Inexpensive portrait figures were made with local Devon clay at Watcombe (Torquay) from 1867 and Doulton made figures, large and small, of celebrities and royalties in the 1880s.

Thimbles There is a great range of gaily decorated porcelain thimbles, those made by e.g. Chelsea or

Derby fetching high prices. Minton, Rockingham and Copeland produced them and they are still made at Worcester.

Tiles Walls have been decorated with tiles for some 3000 years, originally to keep rooms cool in Middle Eastern countries—as they do today in the dairies and larders of northern climes. Moors brought them to Spain and the Dutch brought them to England, in the 16th century. Dutch tiles were of DELFTWARE, hand-painted with all kinds of design from geometrical to ships and Aesop's Fables. One attractive use was to decorate the central stove which dominates many Continental living-rooms.

In England Dutch styles were copied at first, especially at Lambeth and Bristol. Sadler & Green (see LIVERPOOL) specialized in black transfer-printed designs, notably a set of actors and actresses. In the 18th century it became fashionable for the drawing-room to have tiled dados, fireplaces etc. Creamware and other forms of pottery eventually replaced delft-ware.

Interest in tiles revived in the 1870s and they were used extensively in churches, shops, pubs, banks etc. There was a wide range of themes, e.g. Japanese, Burne-Jones, floral, geometrical; sets representing arts and crafts, or Seasons (Minton), months of the year (Wedgwood and Copeland); scenes from Dickens, Scott, Shakespeare. William DE MORGAN also made artistic tiles for William Morris.

Toby jug Generic name for a series of jugs representing a seated figure holding a foaming mug of ale and wearing a three-cornered cocked hat, the crown of which (now usually missing) is detachable for use as a cup (though the jugs were more for ornament than use). The original and most familiar Toby Philpot was supposed to be a Yorkshire toper of fabulous capacity, but many similar jugs represent e.g. Bluff King Hal, Admiral Howe, Martha Gunn (who traditionally gave the future Prince Regent his first dip in the sea at Brighton) and a standing 'Hearty Good-Fellow'; see fig. 114. They first appeared in the 1760s, possibly originated by Aaron Wood (see WOOD FAMILY) but copied by very many others, including early versions in PRATTWARE colouring, and later representations of Nelson, Wellington etc. In the early versions the face is full of character, and the richness of the coloured glazes in the Ralph Wood models is outstanding; late 19th-century copies are without merit.

114 TOBY JUG Squire Toby, Ralph Wood, *c.* 1770 (*City Museum, Stoke-on-Trent*)

Transfer-printing   The decoration of ceramics with printed designs transferred to them by specially prepared paper from engraved copper plates; any number of copies could be taken from one engraving, thus greatly reducing costs (hand-painting being expensive). The process was invented for use on enamel wares at Battersea (1753–56); then it was introduced and adapted for use on porcelain by Robert Hancock (1756) at Bow (where it was little used) and Worcester (where it was used extensively).

At first the transfers were applied over the glaze; the ink, a mixture of enamel colour and printer's ink, was usually grey-black, red or lilac. Claims are made that Sadler & Green (see LIVERPOOL) made even earlier use of black overglaze transfer-printing on pottery tiles; they were so decorating Longton Hall porcelain c. 1760 and Wedgwood creamware soon afterwards.

The commonest form, however, is *underglaze printing*, at first almost invariably in cobalt blue (see BLUE-AND-WHITE); this was introduced at Worcester c. 1759, also by Hancock. The design was applied to the biscuit, fired and then glazed. The practice spread to other porcelain factories, e.g. Caughley (c. 1775), Lowestoft, Liverpool and Bristol, but became the mainstay of the pottery industry after Spode introduced it to Staffordshire c. 1781. Smudgy outlines were an early defect, but in 1806 the invention of a better transfer paper permitted the addition of stipple to line engraving, and increased clarity and finer gradations of tone (fig. 115). Pink, brown and green colours were used from c. 1828, and three colours on a single transfer from the 1840s; but blue continued to predominate. Possibly to pacify artists threatened with redundancy by the process, Spode

115 (*right*)
TRANSFER-
PRINTING Black-
and-white
printed frog mug,
W. Adams &
Sons, 1851; see
also fig. 53
(*Mary Payton
Antiques*)

For man dieth,
and wasteth away;
yea, man giveth up
the Ghost and
where is he.

116 (*left*) WALL
PLAQUES
Sunderland lustre
plaque by Dixon,
Phillips & Co.,
c. 1834–65
(*Sunderland
Museum*)

117 (*right*) WALL
PLAQUES Floral
example in the
style of Thomas
Steele, Derby
c. 1820

among others introduced the overglaze painting-in of underglaze printed outlines. In overglaze printing greater clarity was achieved by *bat-printing*, in which a flexible 'bat' (pad) of glue and treacle was substituted for transfer paper. This was used by Flight & Barr, Copeland and Minton. See also PRATTWARE, LATE.

Turner family (1756–1803) Staffordshire potters at Lane End. John I from 1756 made fine stoneware jugs and vases, often with applied ornament. His sons, John and William, patented the first STONE CHINA (1800).

Wall plaques A ceramic substitute for pictures, pierced with holes to hang on the wall, where they were sometimes, from the 17th to the early 19th century, the only adornment. Oval or rectangular, moulded in low relief and occasionally with an elaborately moulded 'frame', they were made in every sort of material—delftware, creamware and other kinds of pottery, even occasionally in porcelain. They might depict domestic animals, flowers (fig. 117), kings and queens, biblical or historical themes etc. The most familiar are the Prattware ovals (see PRATTWARE, EARLY), often with the same moulded design as the Prattware jugs; and the forbidding Sunderland lustre texts ('Prepare to meet thy God'), sometimes with a name and date added (fig. 116). 'The Sailor's Farewell', with doggerel verse, and transfer prints of Sunderland's Wearmouth iron bridge (1796) were also favourites. Blue-dash chargers (see DELFTWARE) were also made to hang on walls.

Walton school (c. 1806–46) STAFFORDSHIRE FIGURE makers who worked in the tradition of John Walton of

Burslem. He may be said to have brought to the cottage mantelpiece pottery versions of the Derby porcelain groups, adapting their BOCAGES in a characteristic highly stylized form with double leaves (placed back to back) radiating from a coloured flower. Against these stood figures or groups, not only versions taken from Derby and other porcelain factories but from earlier potters (e.g. the WOOD FAMILY); most of these became standard themes for later potters, e.g. the Shepherd and Shepherdess, Gardener and Mate, Huntsman and Mate, the Tithe Pig (see STAFFORDSHIRE GROUPS and Plate 1), Elijah, the Flight from Egypt, and many animals. These often bear titles on the front of the base and, except for early examples, the name 'Walton' on a scroll at the back. They were gaily painted in green, blue, yellow, brown etc., often with dappling on the base.

The best of his followers was *Ralph Salt* of Hanley (worked 1812–46), who sometimes put his name on the back. His bocages were less symmetrical, the spelling of titles bizarre (Shepherdiss, Archar, Sport Man) and he displayed more humour and less sentiment than Walton. The typical base was high, waisted and had an oak-leaf on the front.

One of the large *Tittensor* family, possibly Charles (working *c.* 1815–25), also made bocage figures; the bocages were smaller and carelessly modelled but the colouring was attractive.

Washstand china Sets consisted of ewer and basin, soap-dish, sponge-dish, toothbrush-tray, slop-pail. Colourful sets were made in the 19th century by Minton, Wedgwood and others and are now being bought to use for salads, fruit cups, flower arrangements and the slop-pails for umbrella stands.

Watch-stands Victorian flatbacks with a hole into which a watch (sometimes a clock) could be placed, for use on the bedside table or on the mantelpiece. The flatback might take the form of a castle front, a group of figures etc.

Watering-cans 18th-century versions, complete with saucers and perhaps lids, were about 6 in. (150 mm) high and were used to sprinkle lavender water etc. on porcelain or wax flowers, or to water real flowers growing indoors. Miniature cans made later seem to be merely decorative toys (fig. 118). There is a wide variety, made e.g. by Spode and Davenport, many of them most attractive.

Wedgwood (1759–today) A Staffordshire firm famous for many innovations in pottery manufacture,

119 (*above*) WEDGWOOD/ WHIELDON Cauli- flower teapot. *c.* 1755 (*Wedgwood Museum*)

118 (*left*) WATERING- CANS Royal Crown Derby miniature; Imari pattern, 1918 (*Sotheby's Belgravia*)

founded at Burslem by Josiah Wedgwood. From 1754 he had partnered WHIELDON in developing AGATE, marbled and tortoiseshell wares and a fine deep GREEN GLAZE particularly associated with the table-ware moulded in cauliflower (fig. 119), melon or pine-apple patterns which he later made at his own pottery.

At first Wedgwood made only useful wares at Burslem, but in 1769 he entered into partnership with Thomas Bentley and opened a second factory (and village) near Stoke, named Etruria because the Greek classical pottery recently excavated at Pompeii and Herculaneum was at that time thought to be Etruscan. The Etruria output comprised ornamental wares in the Neo-Classical taste derived from those finds, and here Wedgwood evolved his famous BLACK BASALT (c. 1767) and blue JASPER WARE (1776). Ornamental wares marked 'Wedgwood and Bentley' (1769–80) are of the highest quality. The manufacture of domestic wares continued at Burslem.

From the beginning Wedgwood also made CREAM-WARE; this was called QUEEN'S WARE when he was appointed Potter to Queen Charlotte (1765). Cream-ware table services, with printed patterns and painted borders, were exported in vast quantities to the Continent, where they superseded delft and *faïence*; creamware is still the firm's staple product. Some examples, painted in a free style by Émile Lessore (1858–67) and signed, are much in demand.

Other innovations, often short-lived, were buff creamware with '*Rosso Antico*' (i.e. red) reliefs, 'Moonlight lustre' (pink, with marbled effects in other colours), 'Carrara' (i.e. Parian) figures (1848) and green-glazed MAJOLICA. Bone china was intro-duced in 1812 but, proving unsuccessful, was

120 WEDGWOOD
Fairyland lustre
bowl

abandoned soon afterwards, to be revived from 1878. The London showrooms were closed during a trade recession (1828–75). Wedgwoods, now at Barlaston, still make jasper and basalt wares in addition to bone china and creamware. In the 1920s, series of lustre-ware bowls etc. were introduced: Fairyland lustre (fig. 120; elves and pixies in dreamlands, mixed up with gondolas and Chinese figures), Dragon, Fruit and Butterfly lustres, the names indicating the dominant themes. Almost all products made after 1770 are clearly marked.

Wemyss ware (1880–1930) High-quality pottery made at the Fife Pottery (established 1817) near Kircaldy, by the Heron family assisted by a Czech named Nekola. Vases, mugs (fig. 121), tea-sets, bowls, candlesticks etc. were made, typically painted underglaze with naturalistic fruit or flowers (especially a large pink rose) or a cock-and-hen design in black. Characteristics include fine crazing and a blue-green rim; most pieces were marked. Wemyss ware (named after near-by Wemyss Castle; pronounced weemz) was only a small part of the pottery's output, which was mostly cheap and utilitarian. The production of Wemyss ware was continued by Nekola's son at Bovey Tracey, Devon (1930–57).

121 (*right*) WEMYSS
WARE Three-handled
mug showing cocks
and hens (*Christopher
& Amoret Scott*)

122 (*left*) WHIELDON
WARE Whieldon-type
brown and green
tortoiseshell plate,
c. 1745. Moulded
inscription: 'Success
to the King of Prussia
and his Forces'
(*Willett Collection,
Brighton*)

Whieldon ware (*c.* 1740–80) A convenient label
for Staffordshire lead-glazed earthenware distinguished
from ASTBURY and ASTBURY-WHIELDON WARE in three
respects: greater reliance for decoration on a wider
range of more brilliantly coloured glazes (yellow, blue,
green, brown etc.); the use of an improved cream-
coloured body of the same constituents as the best
white SALTGLAZE (but fired at a lower temperature);
and greater sophistication. Brilliant mottled and

tortoiseshell effects were produced by dissolving the metal oxides in the liquid lead glaze or by dabbing on the coloured glaze with sponges (fig. 122).

Tableware included tortoiseshell plates (relatively common), teapots with crabstock handles and spouts in a paler shade of clay matching the relief decoration but contrasting with the pot itself, jugs, tureens; there were also cottages (with figures), COW-CREAMERS, dovecotes and other new inventions.

Figurines of the earlier types were made, but also others inspired by Chinese or Classical originals, portrait busts of celebrities or fictional characters, early examples of later favourites such as the Lost Sheep, Shepherd and Shepherdess etc. and possibly the earliest of the Toby jugs.

They were made by many Staffordshire potters (e.g. the WOOD FAMILY) but are associated with a leading innovator in this field, Thomas Whieldon (1719–95), who worked at Little Fenton (1740–80) and took on Josiah Wedgwood as his partner (1754–59). The classification (like the other two mentioned) is arbitrary, inadequately defined and subject to erosion as research into this obscure period advances. For example, Whieldon also made agate and Jackfield ware, and saltglaze figures.

Willow pattern A term best reserved for only one type of mock-Chinese blue-and-white transfer-printed pattern found on English pottery and porcelain—that for which the tale was invented of a girl who eloped with her mandarin father's secretary on the day she should have wedded a rich old merchant. The mandarin chased them across a bridge but they escaped by boat to the young man's island home; later they were arrested, threatened with death but, changed by the gods into turtledoves, flew away.

The design shows two fleeing figures on a bridge and usually a third in pursuit; a pagoda, boat, two doves and, top left, the island home; and, prominent in the foreground, a willow and an 'apple' tree. Of the theories about its originator, the most likely seems to be that Thomas Minton who, on leaving Caughley (1785) where he learnt engraving had set up his own engraving shop, drew inspiration from a similar (but bridgeless) Caughley design by Thomas Turner and engraved the first true willow pattern, selling it to various factories, beginning possibly with Spode. It is not found on Caughley wares.

The Willow pattern has proved immensely popular ever since, allegedly copied by 200 potters already by 1865. There are many variants, but the number of people on the bridge or of 'apples' on the tree are uncertain guides to date or factory. There are also many 'willow landscapes' of similar style but they lack some essential features.

Wine and bin labels Pottery bin labels came into use in the 1750s and are still used to identify sections of a well-stocked cellar. The earliest are in delftware; labels made by Wedgwood and Spode are sometimes marked on the back. The vintage year is sometimes given, and there are some amusing names—'Orange Shrub', 'Marcella' (presumably Marsala) and even 'Teneriffe'; the humbler drinks are not forgotten— there is one marked 'Elder Flower'.

Porcelain wine labels are less common than silver, but may be collected; there are more nostalgic names than 'port' and 'brandy', e.g. 'Rhenish'.

Wood family (worked *c.* 1754–1846) A family of

Staffordshire potters at Burslem, famous for earthenware figures and groups. Ralph Wood Senior worked for John Astbury and Thomas Whieldon before setting up on his own c. 1754. His products may be distinguished by their excellent modelling and the use of beautifully lustrous coloured glazes painted on with the brush instead of being dabbed on almost at random in the Astbury-Whieldon tradition (fig. 114). His son, also Ralph (born 1748), worked in the same style at first, and his early products are indistinguishable from his father's except in the rare instances when they were marked; tradition attributes the mark 'R. Wood' to the father and 'Ra Wood Burslem' to the son.

Some authorities think that Ralph I's figures were modelled by his brother Aaron, who had learnt his craft from Thomas Wedgwood and from Whieldon. Another modeller who worked (c. 1770–90) for one or both of the Ralphs was the maverick *Jean Voyez* whom Josiah Wedgwood had had imprisoned for reasons unknown. To him are attributed rather sentimental figures, e.g. the Lost Sheep—a biblical theme much copied in later years; he also originated the 'Fair Hebe' jug (on which a youth offers a girl a nest of eggs). Other tentative attributions are: to Ralph I, Elijah and the Raven; to Aaron, Old Age, the Vicar and Moses (see STAFFORDSHIRE GROUPS) and Hudibras; to Ralph II, rural groups such as Scuffle, Friendship and Tenderness.

From c. 1790 Ralph II began using enamel colours instead of coloured glazes; in this style are portrait busts (Handel, Milton) and figures (Chaucer, Shakespeare, Newton), thought by some to have been modelled by his cousin Enoch.

Ralph II was succeeded by Aaron's son, Enoch, who

founded *Wood & Caldwell* (1790–1818) and Enoch Wood & Sons (1818–46), which made all types of pottery (fig. 123). Enoch had shown ability in modelling as a boy and did his best work before he was 30; this took the form of portrait busts (e.g. one of Wesley, 1781, done from life) which were accurate but uninspiring. He may have originated two widely copied figures: the Night Watchman and the Parson and Clerk. Enoch Wood & Sons also made large quantities of fine blue-and-white printed earthenware, creamware services, jasper, black basalt etc.

Worcester (First Period; 1751–83) The porcelain factory founded by Dr Wall, William Davis and others has continued at Worcester, under various names, down to today. Its most prized products belong to the first period, divisible into the Dr Wall period to 1774, when he retired, and the Davis/Flight period.

Early Worcester porcelain was the finest in England, denser, more thinly and evenly potted and better finished than Bow or Chelsea; unlike most soft pastes, it did not crack under boiling hot tea. The soapstone body, made to a formula bought from LUND'S BRISTOL factory, shows green against the light; the glaze, like Caughley's, never crazed. The absence of glaze round the foot-rim of bases, once used in identification, is not peculiar to Worcester or due to 'glaze shrinkage'; the glaze was cut away round the edge to stop its flowing over it when fired.

The principal wares were tea and coffee sets; moulded tureens, sauceboats, bowls and jugs, often copied from silver models; pierced openwork 'chestnut' baskets; small leaf-shaped pickle dishes etc. Complete dinner services are uncommon, as the soapstone body was unsuitable for large plates; for the same reason figures are very rare (fig. 13). At first most pieces were painted in underglaze blue, with CHINOISERIES. TRANSFER-PRINTING was introduced by Hancock in 1756, at first overglaze, mostly in black, with Hancock's designs of classical ruins, hunting scenes, celebrities (e.g. Frederick the Great) etc. Underglaze blue-and-white printed wares soon followed, mostly with landscape or floral designs, and were later produced in vast quantity; the tone varied from sapphire at first to violet-blue after Wall's retirement, both now darkened with age. Some designs were outlined in black print and coloured with enamels; others were 'pencilled' (painted with very fine brushwork). ARMORIAL services were commissioned by royalty and the aristocracy.

From the 1760s there was much overglaze polychrome (often FAMILLE VERTE) painting of oriental themes, Meissen flowers or European landscapes. Worcester is famous for its ground colours, emulating Sèvres and Chelsea; by 1769 there was a wide range, including powder-blue (powdered pigment dusted on), mazarine, turquoise, claret, a rare yellow, 'apple' (actually, pea) green. These grounds have often been added to genuine Worcester by fakers (see CLOBBERED). Blue and pink grounds were frequently lightened by wiping out the colour in fish-scale, sometimes fish-roe (shagreen), patterns, to form the much prized scale-blue etc. Reserves (i.e. shaped patches of white) were also left in the ground colour and decorated, notably by the Chelsea artists who arrived *c.* 1768, possibly working freelance; they traditionally include O'Neale (Aesop's fables), Donaldson (copies of Boucher) and Duvivier. Many such wares were sent for decoration to the Giles Studio (see LONDON DECORATORS. Kakiemon and, later, Imari designs (see JAPAN PATTERNS) were also borrowed and turned into rich new forms called 'Worcester japans', many with radiating whorled panels.

In the Davis/Flight period, although the old lines were continued (fig. 62), there was a switch to emphasis on lower priced blue-and-white ware with cheaper materials, to meet competition from Caughley and China. The body became heavier and greyish, translucency straw-coloured, glaze blued, bubbled and speckled. Much of this, marked with 'Chinese' disguised numerals (fig. 112), has only recently been proved to be Worcester, not Caughley; the tradition that Worcester decorated Caughley wares (or vice versa) has also been disproved. Many new patterns were introduced, e.g. the 'Fisherman and Cormorant', 'Temple', 'Birds in a Tree'.

In 1783 Davis died and Thomas Flight bought the Worcester factory, leaving its management to his sons. When one of them died, Martin Barr was taken on as partner. See FLIGHT & BARR WORCESTER.

Appendix A

★
USEFUL DATES
(some are approximate)

9th century	First hard-paste porcelain (T'ang Dynasty)
1368–1644	Ming Dynasty
16th century	Chinese porcelain exports to Europe begin to expand
1571	Delftware introduced to England by the Dutch
1575	First soft-paste porcelain, Florence
1643–1715	Louis XIV. Age of Baroque
1657	Tea importation begins
1670–85	Toft's slipware
1671	Stoneware. Dwight's first patent
1673	First French soft-paste, Rouen and St Cloud
1685	Huguenot refugees, after revocation of Edict of Nantes
1688	William of Orange. Dutch craftsmen arrive, e.g. Elers brothers
1690–1850	Nottingham stoneware
1710–today	Meissen
1715–74	Louis XV. Age of Rococo
1718–1864	Vienna
1720	Cream-coloured earthenware introduced
1720	White saltglaze and Astbury figures first appeared
1725–1800	Chantilly
1738–56	Vincennes
1740–50	Astbury-Whieldon figures
1740–80	Whieldon wares
1740–80	Jackfield ware
1745	Rococo reaches England
1745–70	Chelsea
1746–76	Bow
1748	Excavations at Pompeii and Herculaneum began
1748–52	Lund's Bristol. Soapstone porcelain
1749–60	Longton Hall
1749–1848	Derby
1751–54	Girl-in-a-swing factory

1751–83	Worcester, Dr Wall and Davis/Flight periods
1752–56	Chelsea Red Anchor
1754	Ralph Wood Senior began work
1754	Liverpool (several factories opened)
1755–59	Figures with 'bun' bases
1756	Transfer-printing (overglaze), introduced at Bow and Worcester
1756	Prussians took Dresden; beginning of Sèvres ascendancy over Meissen
1756–today	Sèvres (soft paste until 1804)
1757–99	Lowestoft
1758–70	Chelsea Gold Anchor
1758	Figures with rococo bases and bocages appeared
1759–today	Wedgwood
1759	Underglaze transfer-prints, introduced at Worcester
1760–1878	Leeds
1760s	Toby jugs first introduced
1765	Wedgwood Queen's ware first marketed
1767	Wedgwood Black Basalt first marketed
1768–73	Plymouth and Bristol (Cookworthy)
1769	Wedgwood's Etruria factory opened
1770–84	Chelsea-Derby
1770–today	Spode; Copeland & Garrett 1833–47, then Copeland
1773–81	Champion's Bristol
1774–93	Louis XVI. Neo-Classical Age
1775–99	Caughley
1775–1800	Neo-Classical styles predominant on cream-ware and stoneware
1776	Declaration of American Independence
1776	Wedgwood Jasper ware introduced
1779	Wedgwood Pearlware introduced
1780	Mocha ware first made
1780–1835	Early Prattware
1781–1835	New Hall (hard-paste to 1814)
1783–93	Worcester, Flight period
1786–1811	Crown Derby
1786–1852	Chamberlain's Worcester
1789	French Revolution
1790–1820	Castleford

1790–1818	Wood & Caldwell
1790–1830	'Regency' period
1792–1855	Ridgway
1793–1840	Worcester, Flight & Barr etc.
1793–1887	Davenport
1793–today	Minton
1794	Bone china marketed by Spode
1794	Duty on imports from Far East greatly increased
1796–1813	Pinxton
1796–today	Coalport
1799–1893	Don Pottery
1800	Turner's stone china patented
1800–89	Grainger's Worcester
1805	Spode's stone china introduced
1806–46	Walton School
1810	Manufacture of soft-paste porcelain ceased in England and France
1810	Revived Rococo period began
1811–48	Bloor Derby
1813	Mason's Patent Ironstone china introduced
1813–20	Nantgarw/Swansea
1815	End of Napoleonic era
1815–today	Doulton
1815	Felspar china introduced by Spode (1820, Coalport)
1825–40	Madeley
1826–42	Rockingham bone china
1837–1901	Victorian era
1842	Parian ware first made
1846–78	Sampson Smith flatbacks
1847–88	Late Prattware and potlids
1850–1914	Fairings
1851	The Great Exhibition, Hyde Park
1857–today	Belleek
1858–1929	Goss
1861–65	American Civil War
1862–today	Royal Worcester Porcelain Co.
1865	Annual hiring of potters abolished
1870–95	Castle Hedingham
1870–1904	*Pâte-sur-pâte*, Minton
1873–1915	Martinware
1876–today	Royal Crown Derby

1890	Art Nouveau period began
1900	Use of lead in potteries abolished
1920	Art Deco period began

Appendix B

NOTABLE COLLECTIONS
(Museums and country houses open to the public)

Alton, Hants. Curtis Museum
Bedford. Cecil Higgins Art Gallery (18th-century porcelain, especially Chelsea)
Birmingham City Museum and Art Gallery (Wedgwood and porcelain)
Bootle, Lancs. Museum and Art Gallery (Pottery figures and Liverpool pottery)
Brighton Art Gallery and Museum (Willett Collection of pottery figures; Sussex pottery)
Bristol. City Art Gallery (porcelain, delftware)
Cambridge. Fitzwilliam Museum (Glaisher Collection of porcelain, slipware, delftware)
Cardiff. National Museum of Wales (Nantgarw/Swansea and Welsh pottery)
Castle Howard, near Malton, Yorks (Chelsea)
Cheltenham Art Gallery and Museum (porcelain)
Derby. Museum and Art Gallery, Wardwick (Derby and brownware)
Edinburgh. Lady Stair's House (Scottish pottery)
Harrogate. Royal Pump Room Museum (Leeds)
Hastings Public Museum and Art Gallery (Sussex and Kent pottery)
Leeds City Art Gallery (Leeds and Staffordshire pottery)
Lincoln. Usher Art Gallery
Llandudno. Rapallo House Museum
London:
  British Museum
  Fenton House, Hampstead (porcelain)
  Southall Public Library (Martinware)
  Victoria and Albert (Schreiber Collection, pottery and porcelain)

Luton Hoo, Beds. Wernher Collection (porcelain)
Manchester. Fletcher Moss Museum; Heaton Hall, Wythen-
shawe Hall
Melton Mowbray (near), Leics. Stapleford Park (Balston
Collection of pottery)
Norwich. Castle Museum (Lowestoft)
Oxford. Ashmolean Museum (Worcester)
Paisley, Renfrew. Museum and Art Gallery (ceramics)
Plymouth City Museum and Art Gallery (Plymouth and
Bristol)
Port Sunlight, Cheshire. Lady Lever Art Gallery (Old
Wedgwood)
Preston, Lancs. Harris Museum and Art Gallery (Victoriana)
Rotherham, Yorks. Museum and Art Gallery (Rockingham)
Stoke-on-Trent:
City Museum and Art Gallery, Hanley (Staffs. pottery and
porcelain, Mocha ware)
Spode-Copeland Museum
Wedgwood Museum, Barlaston
Sunderland Museum and Art Gallery (Lustreware)
Swansea. Glynn Vivian Art Gallery (Nantgarw/Swansea)
Warrington, Lancs. Municipal Museum (Edelsten Ceramics
Collection)
Wolverhampton:
Muncipal Art Gallery and Museum (pottery)
Bantock House (Worcester)
Wonersh, Surrey. Sharp Collection (teapots)
Worcester. Dyson Perrins Museum, Royal Worcester
Porcelain Co.

U.S.A.

Boston, Mass. Museum of Fine Arts (English pottery and
porcelain)
Chicago Art Institute (Early Staffordshire)
Kansas City. Nelson Gallery of Art (general)
New York City, Metropolitan Museum of Art (English
pottery and porcelain)
Providence, R.I. Rhode Island School of Design (English
figures)

Appendix C

★
USEFUL BOOKS

Pottery

Staffordshire Pottery Figures, Herbert Read.   Duckworth, 1929

English Cream-coloured Earthenware, D. C. Towner.   Faber, 1947

English Delftware, F. H. Garner.   1948

Early Staffordshire Pottery, Bernard Rackham.   Faber, 1951

Staffordshire Chimney Ornaments, R. G. Haggar.   Phoenix, 1955

Victorian Pottery, Hugh Wakefield.   Jenkins, 1962

Victorian China Fairings, W. S. Bristowe.   Black, 1964

A Collector's History of English Pottery, Griselda Lewis.   Studio Vista, 1969

Staffordshire Portrait Figures, P. D. Gordon Pugh.   Barrie & Jenkins, 1970

Staffordshire Salt-glazed Stoneware, A. Mountford.   Barrie & Jenkins, 1971

The Pictorial Pot Lid Book, H. G. Clarke.   Courier (Leamington), 1971

Blue-Printed Earthenware, A. W. Coysh.   David & Charles, 1972

Porcelain

Old English Porcelain (2nd ed.), W. B. Honey.   1948

English Porcelain and Bone China, 1743–1850, **Bernard and Therle Hughes**. Lutterworth, 1955

Victorian Porcelain, Geoffrey Godden.   Jenkins, 1961

English Porcelain Figures of the 18th Century, **Arthur Lane**. Faber, 1961

English Blue and White Porcelain of the 18th Century, Bernard Watney.   Faber, 1963

English Porcelain, (ed.) R. J. Charleston.   Benn/Toronto Univ., 1965

Victorian Parian China, C. & D. Shinn.   Barrie & Jenkins, 1971

Jewitt's Ceramic Art of Great Britain, revised by Geoffrey Godden.   Barrie & Jenkins, 1972

British Porcelain—an Illustrated Guide, Geoffrey Godden. Barrie & Jenkins, 1973

179

Pottery and Porcelain

19th-century English Pottery and Porcelain, G. Bemrose.   1952

The Concise Encyclopaedia of English Pottery and Porcelain, R. G. Haggar and Wolf Mankowitz.   Deutsch, 1957

Looking in Junk Shops (and its sequels), John Bedford.   Parrish/ Macdonald, 1961–

English Pottery and Porcelain Figures, Bernard Hughes.   Lutterworth, 1964

Country Life Pocket Book of China, Bernard Hughes.   1965

Encyclopaedia of British Pottery and Porcelain, Geoffrey Godden. Jenkins, 1966

Animals in Pottery and Porcelain, J. P. Cushion.   Cory, Adams & Mackay, 1966

Antique China and Glass under £5, Geoffrey Godden.   Barker, 1966

The Handbook of British Pottery and Porcelain Marks, Geoffrey Godden. Jenkins, 1968

Commemorative Pottery 1780–1900, J. and J. May.   Heinemann, 1972

Collectors' Pieces series of handbooks on Lustre Ware, Delftware, Staffordshire, Toby jugs, individual factories etc. John Bedford.   Cassell

Individual Factories
(in alphabetical order of factory name)

'Bow', article by Hugh Tait in *English Porcelain*, (ed.) Charleston (see above).   There is no recent book on Bow

Champion's Bristol Porcelain, F. Severne Mackenna.   Lewis (Leigh-on-Sea), 1947

Caughley and Worcester Porcelains 1775–1800, Geoffrey Godden. Jenkins, 1969

'Chelsea', article by J. V. G. Mallet in *English Porcelain*, (ed.) Charleston (see above).   There is no recent single-volume book on Chelsea

Coalport and Coalbrookdale Porcelains, Geoffrey Godden. Jenkins

Derby Porcelain 1750–1848, F. A. Barrett and A. L. Thorpe. Faber

Royal Doulton 1815–1965, Desmond Eyles.   1965

The Pictorial Encyclopaedia of Goss China, Diana Rees and Marjorie Cawley.   Ceramic Book Co. (Newport, Mon.)

The Leeds Pottery, Donald Towner.   Cory, Adams & Mackay, 1963

Liverpool Herculaneum Pottery, Alan Smith. Barrie & Jenkins, 1971

Longton Hall Porcelain, Bernard Watney. Faber, 1957

Mason's Patent Ironstone and related ware, Geoffrey Godden, Barrie & Jenkins, 1971

Minton Pottery and Porcelain of the First Period, Geoffrey Godden. Jenkins, 1968

Nantgarw Porcelain, W. D. John. Ceramic Book Co. (Newport, Mon.), 1948 and 1956 supplement

New Hall and its Imitators, David Holgate. Faber, 1971

Cookworthy's Plymouth and Bristol Porcelain, F. Severne Mackenna. Lewis (Leigh-on-Sea), 1946

Ridgway Porcelains, Geoffrey Godden. Barrie & Jenkins, 1972

Rockingham Pottery and Porcelain, D. G. Rice. Barrie & Jenkins, 1971

Spode, Leonard Whiter. Jenkins, 1970

Swansea Porcelain, W. D. John. Ceramic Book Co. (Newport, Mon.), 1958

Wedgwood, Wolf Mankowitz. 1953

Worcester Porcelain 1751–93, Henry Sandon. Jenkins, 1969

Royal Worcester Porcelain, Henry Sandon. Jenkins, 1972

Appendix D

★

MARKS

(Rare marks omitted)

Bow 1760–76. Painted anchor and dagger on figures (most wares unmarked).

Caughley 'SALOPIAN' or 'Salopian', impressed.
'S', 'So' or 'Sx', blue printed or painted.
'C' (not a cresent), blue printed.
(All these used almost throughout the factory's life.)

Chamberlain's Worcester c. 1786–1810. 'Chamberlains', some with added 'Worcester (Warranted)'.
c. 1811–40. 'Chamberlain's' (with apostrophe), sometimes with a crown or 'Royal Porcelain Manufactory' and a London address.
1840– . 'CHAMBERLAIN & CO.'

1852–62 (Kerr & Binns). Device of 4 script 'W's surrounding a crescent and '51'.
(There were many variations of these marks.)

Champion's Bristol Painted 'X' or 'B', some with a date; painted Dresden crossed swords.

Chelsea and Chelsea-Derby See text.

Coalport 1810–40 (flower-encrusted wares). Script 'Coalport', 'C Dale' or 'CD' monogram.
  1820. Elaborate circular mark with 'COALPORT Felspar PORCELAIN'.
  c. 1830–50. Various marks incorporating 'J(ohn) R(ose) & Co.'.
  c. 1851–61. Monogram of 'CBD' (Coalbrookdale).
  c. 1861–75. 'Ampersand' mark with initials C, S, N in the 3 loops (see text).
  c. 1875– . 'Coalport A.D. 1750', with crown from 1881.

Davenport The basic mark is 'DAVENPORT' with or without an anchor (or crown from c. 1870), in numerous variations. Additions include: 'Stone China' (c. 1805–1820); 'Longport' (mainly after c. 1815); 'Staffordshire' (c. 1870); 'Limited' or 'Ltd.' (c. 1881).

Derby c. 1770–80 (on figures). Script 'N' with model number.
  1786–1825. Crown surmounting a cross with 3 dots on each side and a script 'D' below (incised, or painted in puce, blue or black or, c. 1800–25, red).
  c. 1820–48. Printed 'Bloor Derby', usually with a crown.
  1861–1935 (King Street). The 1786 mark plus initials 'S' and 'H' (Stevenson & Hancock) outside the dots.
  1876–89 (Derby Crown Porcelain Co., Osmaston Road). Crown over monogram of 'CD' with distinctive mark for each year from 1882.
  1890– . 'Royal Crown Derby' over previous mark, plus year mark.

Doulton c. 1820–54. 'DOULTON & WATTS LAMBETH POTTERY LONDON'.
  1854– . Various marks incorporating 'DOULTON LAMBETH'.
  c. 1902–56. Lion on crown (without crown from c. 1922)

over device incorporating 'ROYAL DOULTON ENGLAND'.

1882– (on earthenware, not stoneware). Devices incorporating 'DOULTON BURSLEM'.

Dresden The Dresden crossed swords mark appears on some Champion's Bristol, Worcester and Lowestoft; also (mainly on flower-encrusted wares) on Derby, Coalport and Minton.

Flight & Barr (Worcester) 1793–1807. Incised 'B' or 'Bx'.

1807–13. Crown over 'BFB' (Barr, Flight & Barr); or name in full, without crown.

1813–40. Crown over 'FBB' (Flight, Barr & Barr); or name in full, without crown.

Grainger's Worcester c. 1839–89. 'GRAINGER'; '& Co.' added from c. 1850.

Leeds c. 1775–1878. 'LEEDS POTTERY' or (c. 1790) 'Leeds Pottery' (much copied).

Liverpool Most factories used no mark.
(Herculaneum). c. 1796–1833. 'HERCULANEUM' over crown; 'LIVERPOOL' over anchor.
c. 1822–40. 'HERCULANEUM POTTERY'.

Longton Hall Rarely marked.

Lowestoft c. 1775–90. (On blue-and-white) occasionally, the blue Worcester crescent or Dresden crossed swords.

Mason's Patent Ironstone 1813– . '(MASON'S) PATENT IRONSTONE CHINA', with crown from c. 1815; used also by Ashworths, 1861– .
1813–29. 'G. & C.J. M(ASON)'.
1829–45. 'C.J. M(ASON) & CO'.

Minton Pre-1820. Pattern numbers, usually preceded by 'N' or 'No'.
c. 1824. Several printed marks incorporating 'M' (with pattern name and/or number), or 'Felspar China' or 'Felspar Porcelain'; or 'M & B' (Minton & Boyle, 1836–41) or 'M & Co.' (1841–73) or 'M & H' (Minton & Hollins; c. 1845–68).

1851– . 'MINTON'; from 1873 'MINTONS'; superimposed on world-globe 1863– , plus crown (c. 1873–) plus leaves and 'Est. 1793' from c. 1912.
1951– . Device with 'MINTON FOUNDED 1793'. Distinctive year mark added from 1842.

Nantgarw/Swansea Impressed 'NANTGARW' (often nearly invisible), or 'NANT(-)GARW'.
Painted 'Nantgarw' (often faked, and found on Coalport). 'SWANSEA' (impressed, printed or painted). Often faked if painted.

New Hall c. 1788– (hard paste and bone china). Pattern number in various colours, usually preceded with script 'N' or 'No'.
c. 1815–35 (bone china). Script 'New Hall' in double circle.

Plymouth Occasional symbol for tin, looking a little like a '2'.

Ridgway 1814–30. 'J. & W. R(IDGWAY)' or 'J.W.R.'
c. 1830–41. 'J(OHN) R(IDGWAY)' with a version of the Royal Arms; '& Co.' added c. 1841–55.
1830–55. 'W.R(IDGWAY)(& CO.)'
1862–1904. 'B.W.M. (& CO.)' or 'BROWN-WEST-HEAD, MOORE & CO.'.

Rockingham c. 1826–30. Printed griffin in red (from 1830 in puce) plus '(Royal) Rock(ingham) Works (Brameld)' and/or 'China Manufacturers to the King'. Fakes occur.

Royal Worcester Porcelain Co. 1862–91. Variations of the Kerr & Binns mark (see Chamberlain's Worcester) with crown and last 2 digits of year of decoration, plus (1891–) 'ROYAL WORCESTER ENGLAND' and dots (one dot for 1892, 24 by 1915; then star and dots, and other symbols from 1928).
1867–89. Capital letter denoting year.

Spode 1790– . 'SPODE' or 'Spode', impressed, printed or written.
1800–20. A cross in a circle.
c. 1805–33. Marks incorporating 'SPODE' and 'Stone China', 'Felspar Porcelain' etc.

1833–47. Marks incorporating 'COPELAND & GAR-RETT LATE SPODE(S)'.

1847– . 'COPELAND' plus (c. 1851–85) a fancy version of two Cs interlocking back-to-back.

c. 1847– . Various marks incorporating 'W.T. COPE-LAND & SONS', 'SPODE LATE COPELAND', 'SPODE COPELAND' etc.

Sunderland c. 1799–1864. '(J.) DAWSON (& CO.)'.

c. 1807–65 (Garrison Pottery). '(J.) PHILLIPS (& CO).', 'DIXON (AUSTIN) & CO.', 'DIXON, PHILLIPS & CO.'.

c. 1800–97 (Southwick Pottery). 'A. SCOTT (& CO.)', 'SCOTT & SONS', 'SCOTT BROS.'.

Bell Bros. No mark.

Wedgwood c. 1759. 'Wedgwood' in uneven impressed letters; later 'WEDGWOOD'.

c. 1840–45. 'WEDGWOOD ETRURIA'.

1860– . Sets of 3 letters indicating month and year of production.

Worcester (First Period) c. 1755–83. Blue crescent filled in or cross-hatched (printed wares) or open (painted wares).

c. 1760–75. Blue painted oriental-style marks (on Japan patterns etc.); also found on Bow and Caughley.

c. 1755–75 (on scale-blue etc.). Blue painted square 'seal', with Union-Jack-style design; often faked.

c. 1760–70. Dresden crossed swords, sometimes wth '9' or '91' below.

1774–83 (Flight/Davis). Numbers disguised as Chinese letters.

General pointers to date of manufacture

Post-18th century Royal Arms; *printed* marks (except on underglaze blue).

After c. 1810 Name of printed pattern.

1842–83 (Optional) diamond-shaped *registration mark*, patenting the design. Year letter in top angle till 1867, then in the right-hand angle.

After 1850 'Royal'.

After 1860   'Limited', 'Ltd.'; probably after 1880.

After 1862   'Trade Mark'; probably after 1875.

After c. 1875   'Established'.

1884–   Registration numbers began with 'Rd. No. 1'; reached 100,000 in 1889, 300,000 in 1898, 500,000 in 1908.

c. 1891–   'England'; to conform with the U.S. McKinley Tariff Act.

20th century   'Made in England', '(English) Bone China'.

Most of the information in this Appendix has been extracted, with permission, from Geoffrey Godden's Encyclopaedia of British Pottery and Porcelain Marks.

INDEX